MARCO  POLO

T0148723

FRENCH ATLANTIC COAST

GREAT
BRITAIN

Paris

Seine

Loire

Nantes

Dijon

French
Atlantic
Coast

FRANCE

Lyon

Bordeaux

Rhône

SPAIN

AND.

THE TOURING APP.

shows you the way...
including routes and offline maps!

FREE!

GET MORE OUT OF YOUR MARCO POLO GUIDE

IT'S AS SIMPLE AS THIS

1 go.marco-polo.com/fra

2 download and discover

GO!

WORKS OFFLINE!

SYMBOLS

 INSIDER TIP   Insider Tip

★   Highlight

●●●●   Best of …

☆   Scenic view

☺   Responsible travel: fair
trade principles and the
environment respected

(*)   Telephone numbers
that are not toll free

**PRICE CATEGORIES
HOTELS**

Expensive   over 120 euros
Moderate   80–120 euros
Budget   under 80 euros

The prices are for 2 people in
a double room without
breakfast in the high season

**PRICE CATEGORIES
RESTAURANTS**

Expensive   over 40 euros
Moderate   25–40 euros
Budget   under 25 euros

Price of an average 3-course
meal. Set meals include a
cheap table wine. Eating à la
carte is much more expensive

CONTENTS

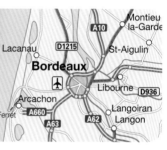

DID YOU KNOW
Timeline → p. 14
For bookworms and film buffs
→ p. 24
Local specialities → p. 28
Force basque → p. 91
Public holidays → 120
Budgeting → p. 127
Weather → p. 128
Currency converter → p. 129

MAPS IN THE GUIDEBOOK
(136 A1) Page numbers
and coordinates refer to
the road atlas

Coordinates are also given
for places that are not
marked on the road atlas

(*A–B 2–3*) Refers to the
removable pull-out map

INSIDE FRONT COVER:
The best Highlights

INSIDE BACK COVER:
Detailed maps of Biarritz,
Bordeaux, La Rochelle and
Nantes

The best MARCO POLO Insider Tips

Our top 15 Insider Tips

INSIDER TIP ▶ **Wafer-thin delicacies**

The crêpes and *galettes* from the *Crêperie de la Fraiseraie* in Pornic come with irresistible, exotic fillings → **p. 44**

INSIDER TIP ▶ **An Englishman on the Loire**

At *Pickles*, the chef is an Englishman, and he delights his French guests with his creative meals → **p. 42**

INSIDER TIP ▶ **Cabanes art**

Strict EU hygiene regulations have led to something very positive. About 20 former oyster farmers' huts in the fishing port at Château-d'Oléron have now been turned into *arts and crafts workshops* → **p. 48**

INSIDER TIP ▶ **Salty ice cream**

The ice cream parlour *La Martinière* in Saint-Martin-de-Ré, the main town on the island, has a number of exotic flavours on offer – such as the mildly salty variety made with *fleur de sel* from the island's own salt pans → **p. 53**

INSIDER TIP ▶ **Paradise with breakfast**

Staying in the small hotel *Blanc Marine* on Noirmoutier is like visiting old friends. The hearty breakfast served by your hosts is wonderful in its own right → **p. 58**

INSIDER TIP ▶ **Sushi in the market hall**

Enjoy sashimi, sushi and California rolls at *Caro Sushi* in the lovely market hall of Biarritz → **p. 88**

INSIDER TIP ▶ **Sweet temptations and ocean views**

At the *salon de thé* of the *chocolatier Miremont* in Biarritz, you can enjoy the most delicious chocolates, cakes and gateaux imaginable in a lovely, old-fashioned ambience → **p. 88**

INSIDER TIP ▶ **River bed**

If you're fond of unconventional places to stay, try the *Bateau Le d'Ô*. This one-roomed hotel is a boat moored on the Erdre, a tributary close to the heart of Nantes → **p. 43**

INSIDER TIP Stand-up paddling: surfers eat your heart out

Anyone who paddles across Arcachon Bay standing up sees things in a very different light. Give this trend-setting sport a try – it's easier than it looks! Paddle to the oyster beds or the Dune du Pilat → **p. 67**

INSIDER TIP Feel like the king of the castle

Château Franc Mayne in Saint-Émilion is beautifully furnished and guests can sample the château's own wines – this is after all Bordelais → **p. 77**

INSIDER TIP Sweet life on a country estate

A work of art of the French way of life has arisen around the award-winning restaurant *L'Atelier de Gaztelur* on a 15th century estate near Biarritz – with an antiques shop, flower-arranging courses and culinary delights in the wonderful landscape of the French Basque country → **p. 87**

INSIDER TIP Walking beside oyster beds

At *Bourcefranc-le-Chapus*, you can stroll through the middle of the famous oyster farming region of Marennes-Oléron (left) → **p. 114**

INSIDER TIP Macarons that are fit for royalty

The delicious almond macarons made by *Maison Adam*, founded in Saint-Jean-de-Luz in 1660, were already served at the wedding of King Louis XIV → **p. 94**

INSIDER TIP Live like Eleanor of Aquitaine

The eight hotel rooms in *Les Jardins d'Aliénor* on Oléron have been individually furnished with loving care → **p. 48**

INSIDER TIP People-watching over *foie gras* and wine

A wine barrel as a table to stand at, delicious *foie gras* (below) with your wine, bustling life around the market hall: time-out at the *Comptoir du Foie Gras* in Biarritz → **p. 88**

BEST OF ...

GREAT PLACES FOR FREE
Discover new places and save money

● *Booty on the beach*

So you still need something for dinner tonight? The tide can give you a helping hand – for free. At low tide, the sea leaves some of its treats on the sand for people to gather quite legitimately. In the meantime, *pêche-à-pied* has become quite a popular pastime along the Atlantic coast → p. 23

● *A view open to all*

It may not be the Eiffel Tower but Gustave worked on this building too. In Arcachon you can climb to the top of the *Observatoire Sainte-Cécile* from where you have a free view over the rooftops of the *Ville d'hiver* and its lovely villas that is green in winter too → p. 66

● *Boating on the Loire*

Boat trips don't have to be expensive. Along the lower reaches of the Loire between Le Pellerin and Couëron and between Indret and Basse-Indre you can take the *ferry* across the river – for nothing! → p. 41

● *Lovely views of the castle in Nantes*

A wonderful view of the Château des ducs de Bretagne can be had for free if you take the 500 m/1640 ft *round walk* along the fortified ramparts. Even if you don't visit the exhibitions inside, you can still get a good idea of the castle's architecture from here → p. 39

● *Visit a wine producer*

Red wine from the Médoc peninsula is world famous. Almost all producers have *wine tasting* arrangements when you can sample the different vintages. Wine tasting is not only informative – it is usually free too, such as in Pauillac (photo) → p. 81

● *Museum visits for free*

Some museums offer free admission on certain days – not to be missed by families. For instance, the excellent *Musée Basque et de l'Histoire* de Bayonne answers all questions about Basque culture free of charge on the first Sunday of every month → p. 90

●●●● Dots in guidebook refer to 'Best of ...' tips

● *Oysters from the farmer*

They don't come fresher than this! Enjoy oysters in the most traditional way possible in a *cabane*, one of the little oyster farmers' huts that have been converted into restaurants such as *Le Relais des Salines* on Oléron. *Huîtres* instead of chips and ketchup is the catchword in such 'snack bars'! → p. 49

● *A stroll around the salt pans*

Coarse sea salt and exquisite *fleur de sel* are must-haves among all the souvenirs to take back after a visit to the west coast of France. The *Musée des Traditions de l'Île* on Noirmoutier shows how the salt is harvested → p. 58

● *Sand and more sand*

Beaches as far as the eye can see are one of the Atlantic coast's most memorable features. Sand *en masse* can be found near Arcachon at the *Dune du Pilat*. Towering more than 100 m/328 ft over the surrounding area, Europe's highest wandering dune has created a unique landscape along the shore (photo) → p. 68

● *Lighthouses*

Rough waters along the Atlantic coast have always been challenging for sea captains, which is confirmed by the many lighthouses. Why not climb up the *Phare de Cordouan* in the Gironde estuary, which has been in operation since 1611, making it France's longest-serving lighthouse! → p. 63

● *White horses*

In the south, huge waves roll in from the Atlantic. Hossegor in particular is a paradise for surfers. Book a course at the surfing school and try your luck – or lie back in your deckchair and watch others struggling to keep their balance → p. 92

● *Desserts and cheese boards*

Every town has developed its own wonderful desserts, and every region has its typical cheese specialities that will turn a picnic into a feast. So: sample and enjoy – e.g. the almond *macarons basques* in and around Saint-Jean-de-Luz, sinful *chocolates* in Bayonne and Biarritz or the variety of cheeses at the *Fromagerie Beillevaire* in Nantes → p. 27, 90, 42

ONLY ON

BEST OF ...

● *Experience life on an ocean liner*
The *Escal'Atlantic museum* in Saint-Nazaire is an exciting place to visit. It makes you feel like you're on board a luxury liner. Explore the different decks and soak up the history of transatlantic passenger ships (photo) → **p. 36**

● *Market magic*
Leave your brolly at home and take a walk around the *indoor markets* in Pornic, Biarritz or Saint-Jean-de-Luz and marvel at the different colours and smells! → **p. 44, 94**

● *Natural goodness*
Water from above the whole day long can spoil things but water all around can put you in a good mood. Treat yourself to a few hours of pampering with seaweed, marine mud and seawater– at *Hélianthal* in Saint-Jean-de-Luz, for example → **p. 94**

● *Stay dry in the water*
Stroll through the fascinating water worlds – and keep your feet dry: sharks, piranhas and a modern, interactive presentation guarantee entertainment at the *Aquarium* of La Rochelle → **p. 54**

● *The Isle of Machines*
You will soon forget the bad weather outside when you visit Nantes' former shipyards. Mechanical sea monsters and other maritime creatures come to life here → **p. 40**

● *World of wine in the Bordeaux*
If you're surprised by the rain in Bordeaux, then spend your time until it stops sensibly at the *Cité du Vin*, where every aspect of wine-growing is explained, and you can also enjoy the fabulous all-round views of the Bordeaux from the panorama restaurant regardless of the weather → **p. 72**

RAIN

RELAX AND CHILL OUT
Take it easy and spoil yourself

● *Herbs and sunlight*
The *Jardin des Plantes* in Nantes with its magnolias, camellias and countless beds of herbs, is an oasis in this lively city. Find your own quiet corner and enjoy the scent of the flowers and the sound of the birds → p. 41

● *Green Venice*
You will only hear birdsong and the sound of the water on a boat trip through the *Marais Poitevin*. Just lean back and let the guide navigate his way through the marshland (photo) → p. 59

● *Relax like Monsieur Hulot*
The best place to relax along the coast is on the beach – even when it's as close to the town as it is in Saint-Nazaire. Just do the same as the main character in *Monsieur Hulot's Holiday* that was filmed here – pack your sunshade and airbed and leave the hustle and bustle of the city behind you on the *Plage de Saint-Marc* → p. 36

● *With the wind behind you and sun in your face*
The flat west coast of France is perfect for gentle bike rides. Don't try to go fast but take in the view instead. Particularly lovely trips can be enjoyed on the islands, such as on *Noirmoutier*. Bicycles can be hired everywhere. There's not a steep hill in sight but a beautiful coastline and shady woods instead → p. 58

● *Gardens of dreams*
You'll find peace and perfectly harnessed nature at the *Planet Exotica* in Royan. Choose your favourite from the Japanese, Mediterranean and tropical gardens, and spend a few hours surrounded by birdsong and the smell of the flowers → p. 62

● *Bathe in Chardonnay – literally*
The combination of wine and therapeutic applications at the spa hotel *Les Sources de Caudalie* in Martillac is balsam for the soul – even if it comes at a price → p. 77

INTRODUCTION

DISCOVER THE FRENCH ATLANTIC COAST!

Burying your toes in the soft sand you gaze out to where the sea and the sky meet on the horizon. Sand yachts whiz along the water's edge and the last sun-worshippers of the day shake the sand from their towels. The clatter of crockery can be heard in the restaurants above the beach where *shellfish* will soon be piled up high on the *étagère* and bottles of chilled white wine uncorked. The proverbial *savoir-vivre* of the French is one of the biggest plus points of any holiday on the Atlantic coast. And the country and the countryside will take care of everything else – seemingly *endless beaches*, clean water, idyllic fishing villages, historical towns and, last but certainly not least, the 500 wine-producing châteaux around Bordeaux.

Variety is the name of the game in this region that stretches from the south of Brittany down across the broad, flat marshlands of the Vendée to the *pine forests* of the Landes département and the rocky coastline of the Basque Country. The first jewel in the long chain of beach resorts is La Baule, a traditional seaside town with a wonderful beach, *beautiful old villas* and the inevitable casino. The islands of Noirmoutier and Yeu further south form part of the adjoining Côte de Lumière. There are no high-rise blocks here, but wide beaches and a *dense network*

They keep anything in view: the *maîtres nageurs sauveteurs* are essential (for survival) at the Atlantic

of cycle paths instead, with pretty hibiscus bushes flowering outside every holiday house and small hotel.

For those who love islands, Île de Ré and Île d'Oléron near La Rochelle are two further places to explore where tout Paris congregates in summer – especially in the case of Île de Ré. Long bridges and causeways – to Noirmoutier, for example – make them easily accessible. Exquisite villas lie hidden among the trees, most of them the *summer houses of wealthy Parisians*. And they come here for a very good reason. The islands, with their unspoilt countryside, *salt pans* and lovely coastlines have a range of gastronomic delights that is on a par with anything in the capital.

The Côte d'Argent merges on the other side of the wide Gironde estuary. It is notable for the endless stretch of wide, sandy beaches and the Landes' forests

56 BC
Caesar conquers Gaul;
Roman settlements founded

5th–8th century
Conquered by the Visigoths,
Merovingians and Caro-
lingians

800
Charlemagne is crowned
emperor. The Frankish kingdom becomes an important
powerhouse in Europe

12th century
The duchess Eleanor of Aquitaine marries Henry Plan-
tagenet who later becomes
king of England. The largest
kingdom in Europe is created through this alliance

1337–1453
The Hundred Years' War

and *lagoons*. The Landes, which start south of the Bassin d'Arcachon, an expansive 57 mi² bay with *numerous types of water sports*, are sparsely populated: There are only 88 inhabitants per square mile – as opposed to the national average of more than 260. This is a flat and huge swathe of countryside where riders and cyclists will find hundreds of miles of bridleways and paths. Many cut through the coastal forests that were planted to stop the wind and the 'migrating' dunes from encroaching on the countryside. The result is the *largest forested area in Europe* covering more than 3800 mi². The different varieties of pines are not just attractive – they are also an important economic factor today on the Côte d'Argent.

South of Capbreton and Hossegor the landscape is different yet again. The Côte Basque is a world of its own: Craggy steep cliffs, the chic *surfer and jet set spa* Biarritz, the pretty harbour town of Saint-Jean-de-Luz, the Pyrenees in the distance, a (second Language that is nothing at all like French, and an ancient culture with *archaic sports* that are lovingly preserved – that's the Basque Country, where the men throw tree trunks, measure their strength chopping wood, and everyone loves playing Pelota.

> **Endless beaches and clean water**

The trading centres of Nantes, La Rochelle and Bordeaux are either on or relatively near the coast and have any number of cultural and historical sights as well as a range of *entertainment and shopping facilities* expected of larger cities. All three owe a considerable portion of their wealth to the slave trade. Glittery trinkets were

1562–1598
The wars of religion bring France to its knees. 1598: the Edict of Nantes – Protestant Huguenots are no longer to be persecuted

1643–1715
Cultural and economic heyday under Louis XIV, the Sun King

1789–99
French Revolution. The liberal Girondists from the *département* of Gironde gain popularity at first but fall victim to the guillotine of the radical Jacobins. Resistance in Royalist Vendée

1914
Bordeaux becomes the seat of the French government in World War I

loaded onto ships in their ports to be exchanged for people in West Africa who were then transported to the Caribbean to be sold. The ships returned to their home ports laden with indigo dye, coffee, sugar and cocoa. The money that such freight brought with it was used to build magnificent palatial buildings.

However, the old towns also demonstrate a sporting and lively innovative spirit. Thanks to the newly-built Nouveau Stade de Bordeaux, Bordeaux was one of the venues for the European Football Championship in 2016. And not only has Nantes survived the demise of its traditional ship-building industry and managed the structural change, but in 2013 the country's sixth-largest city, and the biggest

The home of the most famous red wines in the world

one on the French Adriatic coast, also earned itself the title of *"Green Capital of Europe"* – in acknowledgement of its successful combination of economic growth on the own hand, and care for the environment and a high standard of living on the other.

It was the Romans who first settled here almost 2000 years ago. But even if they did call the southwest coast of Gaul 'Aquitaine' – from aqua – not everything here has to do with water. After all, it was the Romans themselves who showed the locals how to make *wine* from grapes – a circumstance that was to mark the history of this area and the everyday life of those living here for evermore. Trading in wine on a large scale had its beginnings in Bordeaux and brought the city its prosperity – still very much reflected in the architecture of the historic city centre that has since been carefully restored and was declared a Unesco *World Heritage Site*.

Between Royan and Soulac-sur-Mer, the Gironde – the widest estuary in Europe – flows into the Atlantic. The tide of the Gironde reaches 100 km/62 mi into the land. The region on the west coast, the *Médoc*, is home to some of the world's most famous red wines. And of course, this wouldn't be France if the locals weren't also experts in preparing food to match. Fish and seafood characterise menus on the coast, with coveted delights in the form of the controversial *foie gras* or duck breast found further inland.

1940
Bordeaux briefly becomes the wartime seat of the French government

2008–2015
Following several epidemics, breeders along the Atlantic lose 40–100 percent of their oysters. The causes are a bacterium and changes in climate

2013
Nantes is named „European Green Capital"

2016
France reduces the number of its regions; in the southwest, Aquitaine, Limousin and Poitou-Charentes are joined to form the Nouvelle-Aquitaine (capital: Bordeaux)

Sensitivity is the order of the day, but velvet gloves are not required: grape-picking in the Médoc

Despite glamourous seaside resorts such as Royan, Arcachon and Biarritz, the French Atlantic Coast is more *down-to-earth* than most stretches of the Mediterranean. Campsites lie cheek by jowl behind the dunes the length of the Côte d'Argent and the banks of inland lakes are perfect for families with children. Prices here are also much *more family-friendly* than between say Saint-Tropez and Nice.

And with some 500 km/310 mi of beach it is not difficult to imagine why the Atlantic coast is a paradise for *sport-minded holidaymakers*. Waves, sand and wind create perfect conditions for surfing, (sand) yachting and paragliding. Thanks to the rivers and lakes, rafting enthusiasts, anglers and the boating fraternity do not miss out either, and those who are wary of the power of the Atlantic will find *safer places to swim* in the lakes on

> **Variety draws holiday-makers back to the Atlantic**

the Côte d'Argent. Many of these are linked by *courants* – watercourses – and resorts can be found along their banks with *holiday houses*, campsites, small hotels and a comprehensive range of sport and leisure facilities.

It is this variety that draws many holidaymakers back to the Atlantic time and again. And somewhere along this stretch of coastline, with the sand between your toes and fresh seafood on your plate, you're bound to think of the proverbial *savoir-vivre* of the French. And you'll have to agree, there's certainly some truth to that!

WHAT'S HOT

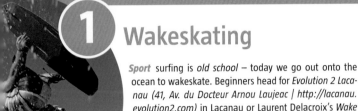

1 Wakeskating

Sport surfing is *old school* — today we go out onto the ocean to wakeskate. Beginners head for *Evolution 2 Lacanau (41, Av. du Docteur Arnou Laujeac | http://lacanau. evolution2.com)* in Lacanau or Laurent Delacroix's *Wake Lagoona (www.wakelagoona.com)* in Virelade near Bordeaux. Lots of wakeshops even have their own teams.

Revue

2

Musical theater Cabaret is enjoying a revival with pomp and feathers, sensuality and humour. Such a colourful spectacle awaits visitors to *Le Saint Sabastien (11, Rue Charles Plumeau | Couquèques | www.saintsabastien.com | photo)* and the *Café Théâtre des Chartrons (170, Cours du Médoc | Bordeaux | www.cafetheatre-chartrons. fr).* And *La Revue de la Cloche (2bis, Rue du Souvenir Français | Saint-Herblain | www.revue-la-cloche.fr)*, 15 minutes from the centre of Nantes, offers classical bright and colourful cabaret.

Don't get up

3

Instead of solid oak ♻ France's furniture-makers opt for a new, environmentally-friendly material. These highly creative people turn paper and cardboard into tables, chairs and cupboards. Amusing furniture and accessories made of cardboard are created at *Cartsandra B (cartsandra-b.fr)* in Peyrehorade. To see just what can be made from this material, check out the blog *100% Carton (www.centpour centkarton.blogspot.com).* To see works by cardboard artist Marie Perrot-Guba and sit on cardboard chairs that are guaranteed to be stable, visit her in her studio *Espace Carton (www.espace carton.com)* near Royan.

RECYCLE

Fish toes

Skin deep Everyone knows the little cleaner fish who live alongside their larger friends in the sea and feed on their parasites and dead scales. This beauty fad runs on the same lines too. If you have a fish pedicure, little fish gently and diligently work away at your feet. The tiny nibblers have long been used in medical treatment to help those with skin problems like neurodermatitis. Such pedicures are available in Bordeaux in *Guily Fish Spa (18, Rue des Bahutiers | www.guily-spa.com | photo)* and in *Ibar of Color (7, Rue Huguerie)*. At the *Secrets Institut (24, Rue Mercœur | www.secrets-institut.fr)* in Nantes, fish is on the programme for both pedicure and manicures.

A sure cut

Fashion Accurate cuts are the trademark of France's latest generation of fashion designers. Marie Rebérat places brightly-coloured fabrics in pleats and drapes for her combinations. At her boutique *(2, Rue Gretry | www.marie-reberat.com)* in Nantes and the branch in La Baule *(5, Av. Pierre Loti)*, the designer also offers creations by other designers. Bordeaux's flagship store Laurie-Anne Fritz *(65, Rue Max Coyne | Le Bouscat | laurieannefritz.com)* also offers pleats, folds and frills. Her designs are easy to wear and yet luxurious. Every December, the fashion scene meets in Bordeaux for the *Salon Ob'Art (www.salon-obart.com)*. To find out more about designs from Aquitaine, go to *Damode Concept – Mode in Aquitaine* on Facebook *(short.travel/fra1)*.

IN A NUTSHELL

AIRBUS

The people on the Côte d'Amour love to bask in the fame brought by the giant jumbo. The aircraft manufacturer Airbus plays an important role in this area. This is primarily due to the workforce of around 2300 in Saint-Nazaire and a further 1800 in Nantes that gave the economically hard-hit region a new impulse after the demise of the shipbuilding industry. Regular guided tours are offered in the summer in Saint-Nazaire. The French Atlantic Coast has always been closely associated with flying. Back in the 1930s, seaplanes were tested on the Côte d'Argent.

OYSTERS

Oysters – in other areas they are a luxury; on the Atlantic coast they are part of everyday life. They are both the passion of those living on the coast as well as an economic factor. The French slurp 150,000 tonnes of oysters year for year. While the oyster beds are covered by water at high tide, it is the *cabanes* that characterise the coastline – huts used by farmers for handling the oysters and where you can often buy the freshest (and cheapest). Apart from their being carefully looked after and handled, the quality and temperature of the water play the most important role in perfecting the taste of the shellfish. Among the best oysters come from Marennes-Oléron near La Rochelle – the richest oyster beds in Europe yielding 40,000 tonnes – and from the Bassin d'Arcachon. The tide also contributes to

Fresh oysters, water, salt and the ocean: four maritime cornerstones of south-west France's self-perception

their quality. Oysters close at low tide. The farmers then climb into the beds to turn the sacks in which the oysters grow – the ones lower down grow more slowly. When the tide is in, the oysters open to feed. It takes between three and four years before an oyster lands on a plate. Up until then, the oyster breeders will have hauled them out of the water up to 20 times, cleaned, sorted and put them back in the oyster beds again. They taste best raw or with a tiny bit of lemon juice.

Ever since 2008, constant epidemics have destroyed first young, then adult oysters. In some place, 50 and even 80 percent of the two- to three-year-old oysters were affected. The Bay of Arcachon in particular was hit by mass mortality. The oyster crisis has not abated. Viral infections and bacteria are causing problems and decimating stocks. Another problem is that the Atlantic is warming up in coastal areas. Environmental pollution is another possible cause of illness. Consumers, however, are not affected as imported oysters make up for the missing quantity. The disease killing the oysters has led to the spread of a new form of criminality: the stealing on a massive scale of healthy shellfish from oyster beds that are then sold to restaurants along the Atlantic coast.

B ASQUES

250,000 Basques live in the Pays Basque region in the southwest corner of France and 2.5 million in the north of Spain. They share a unique language, *Euskara*, that is considered the oldest in Europe. Although there are concerted efforts to promote the language – all signs in the Basque Country for example are in two languages – its survival is still threatened. Not even half the Basques can speak it and it is not taught everywhere in the region. Basque traditions such as the game pelota and archaic tests of strength, however, are carefully upheld, as is Basque architecture. Unlike their fellow countrymen in Spain, the French Basques are not striving for their own independent country but are firmly rooted in France. However, unlike their fellow countrymen in Spain, they were not persecuted under the Franco dictatorship either.

C OURSE LANDAISE

The battle of wits between man and cow that is very much part of the living folklore of *les Landes*, calls for courage and skill, at least on the part of the *torero*. If at the end of this test of strength one of the two parties is injured – or even dead – then, in a *course landaise*, it's the *torero*. He may have a padded pair of trousers, waistcoat and jacket but he is unarmed and has to try to leap out of the way of the charging cow at the latest possible moment. The aim of the game is to demonstrate one's fearlessness and dex-

terity. There are 150 arenas along the coast and further inland and, between March and October, they are bursting at the seams at weekends. For forthcoming events, see: *www.courselandaise.org*.

E LEANOR OF AQUITAINE

You'll come across this lady, known as Aliénor d'Aquitaine in French, time and again on this stretch of coastline. Hotels, restaurants and streets have been named after her. Eleanor (c. 1122–1204) inherited the Duchy of Aquitaine, became Queen Consort of France and England and was perhaps the most dazzling female personality of the Middle Ages. Her biography was correspondingly dramatic and it unfurled on this coast. As no son was born while she was Louis VII's wife, the marriage was annulled in 1152. That same year she married Henry Plantagenet, the Count of Anjou and Duke of Normandy, who was to become King Henry II of England. But these two were also at loggerheads. Henry had numerous affairs while Eleanor held her own court in Poitiers. Under her influence, her sons rose up against their father. Henry crushed the rebellion and had Eleanor imprisoned. It wasn't until after his death in 1189 that she came to power once again, holding onto it until she died in 1204.

T IDES

Every day, ebb and flow along the Atlantic coast cause vast quantities of water to move. Add big storms, and the resulting forces are tempestuous. Erosion has become a very real danger along the Atlantic coast – so real, in fact, that at the surfers' paradise Lacanau, for instance, they are seriously considering moving parts of the town that are on the coast, inland. However, the power

Pilgrims on the Way of St James near Saint-Jean-Pied-de-Port in the Pyrenees

of the tides also has some very positive effects: on the northern coast, in the Breton Département Côtes-d'Armor, the world's biggest tidal power plant for electricity generation was commissioned in 2016. Its turbines, which were sunk into the water without foundation drillings, reliably provide energy with very little environmental impact. Local fishermen chose the location. Greater use is to be made of tidal energy in the future, including along the south of the Atlantic coast.

THE WAY OF ST JAMES

For more than 1000 years pilgrims have been making their way to Santiago de Compostela in Spain where Saint James is reputedly buried. The scallop shell, that has been the traditional emblem of Saint James since the 11th century, can be seen in many churches in Aquitaine. One of the four main pilgrim routes through France that converge in the Pyrenees, leads from Soulac-sur-Mer

at the mouth of the Gironde, down the Atlantic coast to Saint-Jean-de-Luz. The coastal route, also known as the 'English Path' as it was popular among the British as well as the Dutch and Bretons, is the most direct route to the Pyrenees. 550 km/342 mi have now been made into a cycle path.

O Of course, apart from wine, water plays a vitally important role in a region, a large part of which has been known since Roman times as *Aquitaine*. This has led to lots of trendy bars and restaurants being given the name 'O' – the text message abbreviation for *eau*, water. And this is where the 'in' crowd can often be found too – in Biarritz, for example.

PÊCHE À PIED

● Every day at low tide a huge platter of seafood is left on the beach. A mixed bunch of locals and holidaymakers turns up with shovels, rakes and buckets to pick up the mussels, oysters and little crabs for dinner. Check with the Office de Tourisme first about the minimum size of the individual species that you can legally take!

RUGBY

On the Atlantic coast a ball is not always round when it comes to the most beloved pastime in the world. Here, rugby is very much a firm favourite. Many cities in the southwest have several successful rugby teams such as the Stade Nantais Université Club, the Union Bordeaux Bègles, Atlantique Stade Rochelais and Biarritz Olympique. This doesn't mean of course that people are not passionate about football on the Atlantic – which is why you have to practice your pronunciation of 'Allez, les Bleus'!

SALT PONDS

Marais salants, salt evaporation ponds, once stretched all the way from southern Brittany to the Gironde estuary. When the sea retreated over the centuries, the ponds became marshland. Today, salt is once again harvested along the coast. Spicy variants and the precious *fleur de sel* that forms a wafer-thin layer on the surface of the water on hot days only and is scooped up using a wooden shovel, is highly valued by gourmets. The salt ponds have channels that feed saltwater into flat

FOR BOOKWORMS AND FILM BUFFS

Georges Simenon – The Atlantic coast, especially the Côte de Lumière, has inspired many a writer. Georges Simenon (1903–89), who invented the detective Maigret, loved the Vendée and La Rochelle. 15 of his novels are set in the port including "The Hatter's Ghost". Les Sables-d'Olonne provides the backdrop for Maigret on Holiday

Under the sand – Charlotte Rampling stars in this drama directed and written by François Ozon about loss, bereavement and life's deluisions, as a woman whose husband goes swimming and never returns

Pauline at the Beach – This film from 1982 by Éric Rohmer, which is not without its funny side, tells of the teenager's amorous adventures and those of her older cousin, Marion, on the Atlantic coast

Monsieur Hulot's Holiday – The classic comedy from 1953, directed by Jacques Tati, is essential viewing before any trip to the Atlantic coast. The film does with little use of language and conjures up a wonderful holiday atmosphere

Little White Lies – The wind blowing in off the Atlantic coast can be felt in Guillaume Canet's comedy-drama film made in 2010 about a group of friends and couples on their summer holiday in Arcachon. Funny and sad, jovial and melancholy, amusing and never boring – très français in fact

Bicycling with Molière – Philippe Le Guay's 2013 film is about friendship and competition, and is the story of an actor who retired to the Île de Ré. Lovely pictures of the island

Hard graft under the sun: salt worker on the Côte de Lumière

pans that are at slightly different levels. The water, regulated by sluice gates, flows from one pan to the next. A pink coloured crystalline layer forms on the surface, which turns white when dry. The small crystals on the surface form a core around which larger crystals of grey salt are created. This is piled up in the middle of the pan so that surplus water can drain before being shaped into the characteristic pyramid-like mounds around the edge of the salt works, as can be seen in the Vendée and on Noirmoutier and Ré.

WINE

Wine has been grown in the southwest of France since Roman times. After the decline of the Roman Empire it was the monks who kept the happy memory of grape juice alive. Viniculture experienced a big boom following the marriage of Eleanor of Aquitaine to Henry Plantagenet. Through this union a brisk trade was established with England and the Hanseatic League, from which Bordeaux and Bayonne profited in particular. Today, some 8000 *châteaux* around Bordeaux alone – many of the wineries being of a princely dimension – ensure that, at least here, you're going to be pushed for time if you want to sample as many different wines as possible. Bordelais produces 700 million bottles a year, making it the largest wine-growing area at one stretch in the world. First-class wines from the Bordeaux area known throughout the world include the five *premiers crus classés* from the Médoc region's 1500 châteaux: Château Lafite-Rothschild, Château Latour and Château Mouton-Rothschild in Pauillac as well as, slightly further south, Château Margaux and Château Haut-Brion. The scenic Médoc and Haut-Médoc area lies along the banks of the Gironde estuary.

FOOD & DRINK

In France, cooking is considered an art and the production of food a craft that does not tolerate compromises. Apart from the large supermarkets with their first-class fish, meat and cheese counters, traditional bakeries, cake shops, fish, vegetable and cheese specialists and *chocolatiers* all still hold their own. Everything revolves around fresh, unadulterated ingredients, preferably locally sourced. The range of food is dominated by fish and seafood on the coast. The further inland you go, the heartier the dishes – from braised eel to *cassoulet*, a rich casserole from the Périgord region that is given its special flavour by adding duck *confit*. Apart from duck or goose *foie gras* and tender **duck breast** (*magret de canard*), leg of duck (*cuisses*) and duck fillets (*aiguillettes*) are also frequently served. Even the fat and giblets are cooked, such as gizzards (*gésiers de canard*). The tender aromatic flesh is a tasty addition to salads.

Bordeaux is famous for its cep mushrooms that are used in omelettes or served with entrecôtes. Cattle with a particularly tender and tasty meat are bred in Bazas and *les Landes*. **Truffles from Périgord** known as Black Diamonds are a speciality that comes at a price, as it has not been possible so far to cultivate them on farms. Fortunately, just a couple of pieces of a few ounces suffice to give poultry dishes or omelettes that incomparable aroma.

Regional confectionery specialists have a whole range of calorie-rich nibbles at

Oysters, duck and world-class wine: fish and seafood are very much in evidence on the coast as are more hearty dishes further inland

the ready. Try *mascarons nantais*, light **chocolate creations** from Nantes, as well as *rigolettes* that also come from the city on the Loire, *canelés* from Bordeaux, little vanilla pastries with a caramelized crust, and ● *macarons basques*, **almond macaroons** from the far southwest.

The culinary start to the day is light – and sweet. **Breakfast** in hotels and in cafés usually comprises white coffee *(café crème)* with croissants, baguette, butter and marmalade and orange juice.

Supplementing a classic breakfast with ham, a selection of cheese and fruit is no longer anything unusual in medium category hotels. Many hotels down the coast have also expanded their menus to include a variety of egg dishes to please guests from north of the Channel. *Moules frites*, **mussels** and chips, are popular at lunchtime and you will always find a *steak frites* and salads with and without seafood on the menu too. Bars and brasseries have a variety of baguette sandwiches for a quick snack as

LOCAL SPECIALITIES

agneau de pré-salé – especially aromatic lamb grazed on the salt marshes in the Vendée
bordelaise, à la – with shallots, tarragon and red wine sauce, e.g. entrecôte
brébis (des Pyrénées) – sheep's cheese (from the Pyrenees)
chipirons (à l'encre) – squid (in its own ink)
confit de canard – duck preserved in its own fat (photo left)
coquilles Saint-Jacques – scallops
gâteau basque – plain flan-like cake from the Basque Country
huîtres – oysters; the most common are the *fine de claire* variety from oyster farms
jambon de Bayonne – air-dried ham from Bayonne
landaise, à la – prepared to a recipe from les *Landes* region: with garlic and pine nuts sautéed in duck lard

loukinkos – traditional Basque garlic sausage
marmitako – Basque tuna ragout (photo right)
mouclade – mussels in a thick white-wine and yolk sauce, sometimes with curry powder
pipérade – Basque omelette with peppers and tomatoes
plateau de fruits de mer – raw – mussels *(coquillages)* and oysters *(huîtres)* and – cooked – shrimps *(crevettes)*, salt water snails *(bulots and bigorneaux)*, spider crabs *(araignée de mer)*, brown crabs *(tourteau)* – seafood and shellfish on a large platter, the more luxurious variations being with lobster *(homard)* or crayfish *(langouste)*
salmis – ragout in a spicy sauce, e.g. duck *(canard)* or pigeon *(palombe)*
ttoro – Basque fish soup with tomatoes and peppers

well as Croque Monsieur, toasted bread (not baguette) with cheese and ham. Half or a full dozen **oysters** can be found all down the coast, and they are cheap too! They are usually served raw or with a zest of lemon at the most before sepa-

rating them from their shell with a fork and slurping them down.
The most important meal of the day in France is *dîner* that is served between 7pm–9.30pm. It usually consists of several courses and wine is always served

regardless of whether you're in a run-of-the-mill restaurant on the harbourside or in a gourmet temple. The first course is generally *seafood*. But those who don't like fish won't have to go hungry – there are also pastries with herbs, soups and salads, *foie gras* from fattened geese *(d'oie)* and duck *(de canard)* – and snails. The main course could by a perfectly cooked entrecôte *(saignant,* rare, *à point,* medium, or *bien cuit*, well done), lamb, eel braised in red wine or Cognac or *poisson du jour,* fish of the day – either from the ocean or from a lake.

You have a choice from a whole range of delicious *goat's cheeses* afterwards, including various blue cheeses and regional specialities such as Jonchée, a cream cheese made from cow's milk produced around Rochefort. Then there are the sweet temptations: classics such as *mousse au chocolat* or local delicacies like *broyé du Poitou,* a crisp biscuity cake sprinkled with flaked almonds that is not as light as it looks due to all the butter in it.

The most important drink at mealtimes in this region is, of course, wine, preferably from Bordelais. The famous reds (clarets) are produced in *Médoc and Saint-Émilion*; excellent whites in the Loire valley and the Entre-Deux-Mers region southeast of Bordeaux. In the case of whites, the sweet wines should also be mentioned here that are the perfect accompaniment to desserts and cheese, but also unfurl their full flavour with *foie gras.* The most famous is *Sauternes* that is made from the Sémillon grape harvested late in the season.

Pineau des Charentes from the region Poitou-Charentes is particularly famed as an *aperitif,* and consists of three-quarters sweet grape must and one quarter cognac. However, it

The sweet ones accompany desserts and cheese, the dry ones are perfect with *fruits de mer*: white wines from the Bordelais

is also delicious as a dessert wine, for instance with melon and other fruit. The 308 mi^2 of the growing area of *Cognac* in the hinterland of Royan reach as far as the Atlantic coast. Although it is served mainly as a digestif after meals, it is becoming increasingly popular as an aperitif.

SHOPPING

Looking around and shopping at the colourful markets, in pretty shops or at the local wine-producers' themselves are a real pleasure. Normal opening hours in this region are Mon–Sat 10am–7pm. In villages and small towns most places close for a lunch break; in the holiday resorts boutiques and shops usually stay open all day and are often open longer in the evenings and on Sundays too.

Evening markets (7pm–10pm) are held along the coast in the high season, selling crafts, local specialities and clothes. Antique shops are also well worth visiting as are craft workshops. Things may not be cheap but are unusual and well made.

CHILDREN'S CLOTHES

Children's clothes in France are often cheaper, more imaginatively designed and prettier than in many other countries. Certain brand names considered exclusive outside France are quite normal here, e.g. children's underclothing from Petit Bateau is not only sold in boutiques but also in department stores like Monoprix and *hypermarchés* such as Leclerc – and that can be seen in the

prices. The Du Pareil au Même (DPAM) label, e.g. in Nantes, Saint-Nazaire, La Rochelle, Royan, La-Teste-de-Buch, Anglet, Dax and Bordeaux, is very popular and good value.

FASHION

Most Parisian fashion labels can also be found in the coastal towns and in Nantes, La Rochelle and Bordeaux, although prices are not necessarily any lower. Summer sales, however, still exist in France – and from around the beginning of the school holidays real bargains can be found.

In surfer eldorados such as Hossegor and Biarritz you can deck yourself out with brightly-coloured sportswear. Surfing gear and leisurewear such as hoodies, jeans and fleeces from the Australian brand Billabong (which has its European headquarters in Hossegor) or stylish flip-flops from Ipanema can be found in boutiques near the beach everywhere.

FOOD

Shopping and food go hand in hand on the Atlantic coast. The markets and fan-

At the market or the wine-maker's – here you'll find a wide range of things for your wardrobe, larder or cellar

tastic delicatessens make sure of that. And not only chocoholics will feel they are in heaven at a *chocolatier*. Handmade chocolate may not be a very suitable souvenir in summer but it is all the more enjoyable on the spot. Coarse sea salt or the fine-grained delicate *fleur de sel* from the salt farms on the Guérande peninsula or from one of the islands on the other hand is easy to pack and to transport.

KITCHEN ACCESSORIES

Things for the kitchen also make nice souvenirs, from china egg-cups and coffee bowls with maritime patterns to tea towels and aprons – with Breton motifs in the north or traditional bright stripes on the Côte Basque. These stripes also decorate tablecloths, napkins and cushion covers and can be found in boutiques in Biarritz, Bayonne and Saint-Jean-de-Luz, as well as in many villages in the Basque Country.

MUSIC

When looking for music, look out for the independent label Vicious Circle Records, which comes from the city of Bordeaux and is dedicated to artists in the region, such as the band Calc. Mélanie Valéra of Bordeaux is also one of the company's discoveries. In the past few year she has brought out a number of electropop albums under her performing name 'Tender Forever', such as 'The Soft and the Hardcore', 'Wider' and 'Where we are from'. These are distributed by Vicious Circle and keep their magic long after your holiday is over.

WINES & SPIRITS

You can try wine at wine producers' and then fill up your boot. Excellent wines can be found in the Loire Valley, in Bordelais, Pineau des Charentes and Cognac in the Charente area inland from the Côte de Lumière.

CÔTE D'AMOUR

Historically speaking, this section of the French Atlantic Coast belonged to Southern Brittany for many centuries.

Today, the département Loire-Atlantique comes under the administration of the Pays-de-la-Loire region, but the Breton heritage is still very much alive in the minds of the locals. Apart from Nantes, which was once the capital of Brittany, the traditional resort La Baule and the port Saint-Nazaire also belong to the same region. Salt has been harvested on the Guérande peninsula for centuries. It is gathered between June and September, but the salt evaporation ponds can be visited the whole year round. The Côte d'Amour is also known for its idyllic fishing villages sheltered in rocky coves. The strip of coast beyond the Loire estuary is called the Côte de Jade. It reaches down to Pornic.

LA BAULE

(136 A2) (*A3*) The little town of ⭐ La Baule (pop. 16,000) located on the Guérande peninsula evolved into a seaside resort at the beginning of the 20th century when wealthy Parisians had villas built similar to those of spas in Normandy. A stroll past the villas from the 1880s to the 1950s is like a quick *tour de France*, with houses in the style of the Basque Country, Normandy and Provence lining the lovely bay. And of course lots of hotels. 2000 buildings are listed and contribute to the appeal of this town, togeth-

Rocky bays and fishing villages, a fashionable seaside resort and the salt ponds around Guérande – the "coast of love" is full of variety

er with its almost 10 km/6.2 mi-long fine sandy beach and an extensive range of leisure and sports facilities.

SIGHTSEEING

MUSÉE AÉRONAUTIQUE PRESQU'ÎLE CÔTE D'AMOUR

(Not only) for technology freaks and nostalgics: flying machines from the early days of aviation to today. *Aérodrome de la Baule | July/Aug daily, otherwise Mon and Wed–Sat 2pm–6pm | www.mapica.org*

FOOD & DRINK

LE BILLOT

This pretty restaurant with the sunny terrace offers oysters and very well-prepared fish dishes as well as meat. *Closed Sun/Mon | 17, Av. du Pétrels | tel. 02 40 60 00 00 | le-billot.fr | Moderate*

CASTEL MARIE-LOUISE

Top cuisine by Eric Mignard with a regional focus in the eponymous hotel. A three-course meal is served for 39 euros in the evenings from Monday until Thursday. *Except Sun (July/Aug Sat/Sun) closed noon | 1, Av. Andrieu | tel. 02 40 11 48 38 | www.castel-marie-louise.com | Expensive*

There are very many boutiques along the Av. du *Général de Gaulle*. The *market (Tue–Sun, July/Aug and school holidays*

What a wonderful experience: horseback rides along the miles long beach of La Baule

LA CROISETTE

Very pretty brasserie with a terrace around the corner from the central Place du Maréchal Leclerc. *Daily | 31, Place du Maréchal Leclerc | tel. 02 40 60 73 00 | www.lacroisette.fr | Budget*

GRAIN DE FOLIE

Offers very good market-fresh cuisine beside the ocean, prepared and presented with plenty of imagination. There's a different menu every two days! The restaurant is in fact in Pornichet, but is still on the same beach as La Baule. *Closed Sun evening | 150, Blvd. des Océanides | tel. 02 40 61 04 04 | www.grain2folie.fr | Budget–Moderate*

daily from 9am–1pm | Av. des Ibis/Av. du Marché/Av. de Noirmoutier) sells salt, crafts and souvenirs, and you can enjoy oysters with a glass of wine. Try the INSIDER TIP *caramels au beurre salé*, the combination of sweet caramel and salted butter is irresistible!

SPORTS & ACTIVITIES

All the facilities expected of a large seaside resort can be found here, ranging from all types of watersports to cycle hire and riding. There is a golf course in La Baule itself and in Guérande, Le Croisic, Mesquer and Saint-André-des-Eaux. Thalassotherapy is offered at *Centre de Thalassothérapie. Thalgo La Baule*

(Av. Marie-Louise | tel. 02 40 11 99 99 | www.thalasso-barriere.com), the *Relais Thalasso Baie de La Baule (1, Av. Léon Dubas | tel. 02 40 60 80 80 | www.thalasso-tourelles.com) in Pornichet* and the *Spa de la Bretesche (Domaine de la Bretesche | tel. 02 51 76 86 96 | www.bretesche.fr)* in Missillac.

ENTERTAINMENT

Popular clubs include *Villa La Grange (Chemin de la Nantaise)* and *L'Indiana Club (Esplanade Lucien Barrière)* in the casino.

WHERE TO STAY

HERMITAGE BARRIÈRE

One of the most elegant hotels in the town – or, rather, on the beach. A heated seawater pool, sauna and gym mean you are independent of the weather. *200 rooms | 5, Esplanade Lucien Barrière | tel. 02 40 11 46 46 | www.hermitagebarriere.com | Expensive*

VILLA CAP D'AIL

Built in 1927, just 100 m/328 ft from the beach, this villa has individually furnished rooms and a lovely garden. *22 rooms | 145, Av. Maréchal-de-Lattre-de-Tassigny | tel. 02 40 60 29 30 | www.villacapdail.com | Moderate*

INFORMATION

8, Place de la Victoire | tel. 02 40 24 34 44 | www.labaule.fr

WHERE TO GO

LE CROISIC (136 A2) (𝑚 A3)

This pretty fishing port and marina (pop. 4000) is a popular holiday destination. It is located at the end of a peninsula, 10 km/6.2 mi west of La Baule.

Although the coastline and beaches are rocky, sandy bays are exposed at low tide. The *Océarium du Croisic (Av. de Saint-Goustan | July/Aug daily 10am–8pm, mid April–June 10am–7pm, Feb–mid April and Sept/Oct 10am–1pm and 2pm-7pm, Nov/Dec 2pm–7pm | www.ocearium-croisic.fr)* presents marine flora and fauna as an exciting journey into the underwater world – and feeding the penguins *(daily 11am, 3pm and 5pm)* is a terrific experience for families with children.

The elegant hotel *Le Fort de l'Océan (9 rooms | restaurant Sept–June Mon/Tue, July Mon–Thu closed midday | La Pointe du Croisic | tel. 02 40 15 77 77 | www.hotelfortocean.com | Expensive)* at the tip of the peninsula has a tea salon, and offers a guest shuttle service to the restaurants in the town. Ferries to the islands Belle-Île, Houat and Hœdic depart from the harbour *(www.navix.fr)*. Information: *6, Rue du Pilori | tel. 02 40 23 00 70 | www.tourisme-lecroisic.fr*

MARCO POLO HIGHLIGHTS

⭐ **The Escal'Atlantic adventure museum in Saint-Nazaire**
Journey through time back to the era of the transatlantic steamers → p. 36

⭐ **La Baule**
Fabulous villa architecture in this traditional coastal resort → p. 32

⭐ **Les Machines de l'Île**
What is an elephant doing in the middle of Nantes?! p. 40

⭐ **Pornic**
Beautiful coastal town with a harbour and coast paths with lovely views p. 44

GUÉRANDE (136 A2) (*A3*)

The salt capital (pop. 16,000) lies 6 km/3.7 mi north of La Baule. The medieval town wall with its towers and gateways is impressive. *Fleur de sel*, the best quality sea salt, is harvested in the salt evaporation ponds. The ponds and exhibition are open to visitors: *Terre de Sel (Route des Marais Salants | Pradel | Mid Jun–Aug several themed guided tours a day (detailed overview on the website) | www.terredesel.fr).* Also of interest is the *Musée du Pays de Guérande (Porte Saint-Michel | currently being converted)*, which explains the history of the town and region over three floors in one of the three town gates.

An especially 'green' hotel built using ecologically-sound materials is 🌐 *Econuit (70 rooms | 1, Rue du Milan Noir | tel. 02 40 45 85 47 | www.econuit.com | Budget)*. Information: *1, Place du Marché au Bois | tel. 08 20 15 00 44 (*) | www.ot-guerande.fr*

PARC NATUREL RÉGIONAL DE BRIÈRE (136 A–B2) (*A–B3*)

Guided boat trips are available through the marshlands of this nature reserve that covers 190 mi², starting in Crossac Mine, Bréca or Saint-Lyphard. There are INSIDER TIP two excellent restaurants offering regional specialities (such as eel in a salt crust) in or near *Saint-Lyphard*: *Auberge de Bréca (closed Sun evening and Mon | Bréca | tel. 02 40 91 41 42 | www.auberge-breca.com | Moderate)* and *L'Auberge Les Typhas (closed Sun evening mid-Nov–March | Rue du Vignonnet | tel. 02 40 91 32 32 | www.les-typhas.fr | Moderate)*. Information: *Village de Kerhinet | Saint-Lyphard | tel. 02 40 66 85 01 | www.parc-naturel-briere.com*

PIRIAC-SUR-MER (136 A2) (*A3*)

Artists and writers used to spend their holidays here in the olden days. Today, this little village (pop. 2300) 18 km/11.2 mi to the northwest is an idyllic, family-friendly resort with bays for swimming set against a backdrop of pines. On Thu evenings in summer an art and craft market is held on the Place de l'Église. Information: *7, Rue des Cap-Horniers | tel. 02 40 23 51 42 | www.piriac.net*

PORNICHET (136 A2) (*A3*)

Family-friendly seaside resort (pop. 10,000) with three beaches on the eastern side of La Baule Bay. The 4 km/2.5 mi-long *Plage Libraires,* that slopes gently, is particularly popular. The elegant old façades and the casino testify to Pornichet's history as a holiday resort. Thalassotherapy is offered in the *Thalasso & Spa Valdys (66, Blvd. des Océanides | tel. 02 52 56 00 11 | www.thalasso.com/thalasso/les-destinations/baie-de-la-baule)*. Information: *3, Blvd. de la République | tel. 02 40 61 33 33 | www.pornichet.fr*

SAINT-NAZAIRE (136 B2) (*B3*)

Saint-Nazaire (pop. 69,000) is 14 km/8.7 mi to the east of La Baule, right on the Loire estuary, which is spanned by a spectacular bridge. The town is first and foremost a port, shipyard and home to the Airbus works but also boasts 20 beaches. A statue of Monsieur Hulot on the ● *Plage de Saint-Marc-sur-Mer* is a reminder that Jacques Tati made his famous film here in 1953.

The ★ ● adventure museum *Escal' Atlantic (April–June and Sept/Oct Mon–Sat 10am–1pm and 2pm–6pm, July/Aug daily 10am–7pm, Nov/Dec Sun, Christmas holidays daily 10am–1pm and 2pm–6pm | www.saint-nazaire-tourisme.com)* is fascinating, a reproduction of a transatlantic steamer, in the former submarine harbour, like the ones that used to cross the Atlantic from Saint-Nazaire to America in the 1920s and

1930s. The cabins, bridge and promenade decks are all exactly as they would have been back in the day. There are also 200 original items from ships that were built in Saint-Nazaire, ranging from silver tableware to wall panellings.

Something that aviation enthusiasts must not miss is the Airbus factory *(tel. 02 28 54 06 40)* on the harbour. The items that are constructed here include the fuselage of the A380. You must book for the guided tours, which are only available in French. English tours

The elegant Pont de Saint-Nazaire spans the wide mouth of the Loire

The harbour was built by the Germans in 1941 during the occupation of France using a colossal 17,500,000 ft³ of cement. Attempts by the Allied Forces to bomb it, resulted in 90% of the town being destroyed. Three chambers inside the bunker have since been turned into rooms for events. The bunker is crowned by a dome that has come from Tempelhof Airport in Berlin and was used to protect the radar unit up until 2003. Another sight is the 78 m/255.9 ft *submarine Espadon (opening times as at Escal'Atlantic)*, which was launched in Le Havre in 1958. Over its 25 years of service it spent almost 34,000 hours under water, and today is the only museum submarine in France that is not on dry land.

are offered in July and August (book at least 48 hours in advance, but ideally much earlier as they fill up quickly, and bring your passport or other form of ID with you). In July/August, some tours around the STX France shipyard are held in English. Depending on the work in hand, you can watch huge passenger ships being assembled in the dry dock from the gallery. Fish, seafood and ocean views, and during the weeks affordable lunchtime menus are served at the restaurant ⚓ *La Plage de Monsieur Hulot (daily / 37, Av. de Commandant Charcot | tel. 02 40 91 76 17 | restaurant-plagehulot.com | Moderate*) in Saint-Marc-sur-Mer. Information: *Blvd. de la Légion d'Honneur | tel. 02 40 22 40 65 | www.saint-nazaire-tourisme.com*

NANTES

LA TURBALLE (136 C3–4) (*ID A3*)

This little fishing village (pop. 4000) 13 km/8.1 mi northwest of La Baule has a lovely sandy beach and a lively harbour that is famous for the sardines that are brought to shore here. The *market hall (Espace Garlahy)* offers fish and other items on Wednesdays and Saturdays. In July and August, it's also well worth visiting the evening *Art and crafts market (Wed 7pm–9pm | Quai Saint-Pierre)*. The sailing boat Au Gré des Vents, built in 1664, is part of the museum *La Maison de la Pêche (Port de La Turballe | July/Aug daily 9.30am–12.30pm and 2pm–6pm, and Tue–Sat 10am–12.30pm and 2pm–5pm | musee-laturballe.fr)*. Information: *Place Charles de Gaulle | tel. 02 40 23 39 87 | www.tourisme-laturballe.fr*

NANTES

MAP INSIDE BACK COVER
(136–137 C–D3) (*ID C3–4*)
Nantes (pop. 285,000), once the capital of Brittany, lies at the confluence of the Loire, Erdre and Sèvre.

With its cathedral, medieval quarter and the Castle of the Dukes of Brittany, Nantes has always been one of the loveliest, albeit often wrongly overlooked, cities in France. It is hardly noticeable today that the decline of its shipbuilding industry plunged the city on the Loire estuary into a serious crisis. Nantes managed to make the structural change, and has turned itself into a modern, lively metropolis. Its successful combination of economic growth with environmental care and a high quality of life earned the city the title of "European Green Capital" in 2013: with its flawlessly functioning public transport system, numerous environmentally neutral construction projects and green urban development, it is something

WHERE TO START?
Car drivers should head first to the **Place du Commerce** and park their cars in the multi-storey car park. Pedestrians can take the tram lines 1 and 3 to the Place du Commerce. This medieval quarter, the cultural quarter Quartier Graslin and the Île Feydeau are within easy walking distance from here and contain the city's main sights. You can take a water taxi ("Navibus") to Trentemoult from the Gare Maritime, and tram line 1 for the attractions of the Île de Nantes to the Chantiers Navals stop.

of a beacon of excellence. Exciting museums, excellent restaurants and lovely shops reflect this high standard.

SIGHTSEEING

CATHÉDRALE SAINT-PIERRE-ET-SAINT-PAUL

At 37.5 m/123.03 ft the nave is higher than that of Notre-Dame in Paris. The façade dates from the late Middle Ages; the external pulpit is an unusual feature. The stoups made of shells from the Indian Ocean in the Late Gothic interior are noteworthy, as is the Renaissance tomb (that has been empty since the Revolution) of the last Breton Duke, François II and his wife Marguerite de Foix, made of black-and-white marble. Their daughter Anne, whose portrait has also been chiselled out of marble, became Queen of France and is buried in Saint-Denis near Paris. However, her heart found its final resting place in the *Crypt (July/Aug daily from 10am–7pm, otherwise book at Tourist information)* of the cathedral. The cathedral was seriously damaged by fire in

2015. *Place Saint-Pierre | daily 8.30am–6pm, in summer until 7pm | www.cathedrale-nantes.cef.fr*

CHÂTEAU DES DUCS DE BRETAGNE

The seat of the Dukes of Brittany was built from 1466 onwards as a fortress and residence. Following the marriage of Anne de Bretagne with Charles VIII it became the Breton palace of the French royal family. It was rebuilt in the Classicist style after a fire in the 17th century. The ● ✂ walk along the ramparts and to the towers offers a lovely view of both the Old Town and the new city. The ducal apartments are home to the *Urban History Museum (mid June–Aug daily from 10am–7pm, Sept–mid June Tue–Sun 10.30am–6pm)* with the multimedia, audio-visual and interactive history of *Nantes and Brittany. 4, Place Marc Elder | www.chateaunantes.fr*

ÎLE FEYDEAU

In 1926–42 the lower section of the Erdre and several tributaries of the Loire were filled in, which meant that Île Feydeau – that was shaped like a ship – was no longer an island. In the 18th century, the wide streets and shipowners' villas with their carved mascaron ornamentation (faces) turned this district into the most modern in the city. All the buildings have now been restored. On the edge of the

The building of Nantes cathedral took almost 500 years to complete

former island, on Cours Olivier de Clisson, a plaque marks the *house where Jules Verne (1828–1905) was born*. It is not open to the public. The author spent the first eight years of his life in Nantes. *Allée Duguay Trouin/Quai Turenne*

ÎLE DE NANTES AND LES MACHINES DE L'ÎLE

Several bridges link the city with the *Île de Nantes,* which is some 5 km/3.1 mi long and 1 km/0.6 mi wide and washed by two arms of the Loire. In the olden days it was the centre of the maritime trade and shipbuilding. Since the turn of the millennium it has been planted up – to create the *Parc des Chantiers* among others – and given a new lease of life.

A district has evolved that has not only attracted businesses but residents too. Contemporary architecture has found a where mechanical sea monsters congregate as one might expect to find '20,000 leagues under the sea'.

The *Grand Éléphant* is the star in the weird and wonderful Machines de l'Île

foothold here as has avant-garde culture that fits in well among relicts from the industrial era, such as the crane from the 1960s. The island's most popular attraction is the 12 m/39.4 ft-high *Grand Éléphant* that can carry up to 45 people on a 🔅 viewing platform on its back. Its mechanical moving parts are fascinating: its ears flap, the trunk moves and even sprays water and it can blink. All its movements are based on those of a living animal. Steered by a driver, the elephant can carry visitors and locals at 4 km/h/2.5 mph from the banks of the Loire to the machine gallery in a former shipbuilding hangar

The elephant is part of the project ★ ● *Les Machines de l'Île (Blvd. Léon Bureau | very staggered times see website, main time daily 2pm-5pm, April–Oct 10am–5pm/6pm/7pm | www.lesmachines-nantes.fr)*, which also includes the Galerie des Machines. The former shipyard buildings are home to fabulous mechanical works: octopus, giant fish, a storm-battered boat, a horse-drawn carriage, sea snakes. Visitors can use the machines like carousels, and watch them being constructed in the studio. Outside the gallery, the *Mondes Marins*, a 25 m/82 ft tall carousel, is another attraction. *L'Arbre aux Herons*, a 35 m/114.8 ft tall tree with two vast herons, was due to open in 2016. However, the city had to postpone the project due to financial constraints. Instead, the *Café de la Branche* opened under the prototype of the heron tree. Plans for the project that are reminiscent of Leonardo da Vinci's drawings and a model can already be seen in the gallery. An exhibition documenting the redevelopment of the island is housed in *Hangar 32 (32, Quai des Antilles | Fri–Sun 2pm–6pm | www.iledenantes.com).*

JARDIN DES PLANTES ●

17 acres bursting with medicinal plants, camellias and magnolias. *Entrances on Blvd. Stalingrad and Place Sophie Trébuchet | daily 8.30am–8pm, winter until 5.30pm, greenhouses Mon–Fri 12.30pm–6pm, Sat/Sun 9.30am–6pm*

MÉMORIAL DE L'ABOLITION DE L'ESCLAVAGE

The memorial to the abolition of slavery on the banks of the Loire by the Anne-de-Bretagne bridge recalls Nantes' heritage as a former slave trading centre. However, the memorial path is also intended to heighten awareness of modern forms of slavery. It consists of 2000 glass floor tiles in memory of ships and expeditions that set off from Nantes to buy and sell people. There is a stairway down to a display area that features the declaration of human rights, the word "freedom" in 50 languages, and various facts and figures about slavery. *Quai de la Fosse/ Passerelle Victor Schoelcher | daily 9am–6pm, mid-May–mid-Sept until 8pm | memorial.nantes.fr*

MUSÉE D'ARTS DE NANTES

One of the loveliest art collections in France with masterpieces by Jean-Auguste-Dominique Ingres, Gustave Courbet, Marc Chagall, Pablo Picasso and Wassily Kandinsky. At the time of going to press, the extension *Le Cube* was about to reopen on completion of the building works. *2, Rue de l'Hôtel de Ville | daily 11am–7pm, Thu until 9pm*

MUSÉE JULES VERNE

The villa on the hill Sainte-Anne houses letters by the author who was born in 1828 in Nantes and manuscripts of his famous adventure stories. Next to the museum is a sculpture of Verne as a child sitting peacefully on a bench beside his creation Nemo. *3, Rue de l'Hermitage | July/Aug daily 10am–19pm | Sept–June Mon and Wed–Sat 10am–12pm and 14pm–18pm, Sun 14pm–6pm*

INSIDER TIP ▶ TRENTEMOULT

Trentemoult on the southern bank of the Loire was once home to fishermen and seafarers who sailed around Cape

Horn. Today, the former village is a trendy residential area with a marina and good restaurants. A shuttle boat *(navibus Loire)* goes to the Gare Maritime every 20 minutes.

FOOD & DRINK

BATEAUX NANTAIS ✂

Eat with a view of the river! The city disappears behind you to be replaced by country homes and châteaux. Good food is also served during this 2-hour trip on the Erdre. *Daily |Quai de la Motte Rouge | tel. 02 40 14 51 14 | www.bateaux-nantais. fr | Expensive*

LA CANTINE DU VOYAGE ✂

Timeless, extremely relaxed restaurant with chill-out area in a hangar. Diners sit at long tables and have the choice of two inexpensive meals. There are deckchairs where guests can enjoy the views of the sunset and of Nantes before or after their meal. No reservations! *daily | 20, Quai des Antilles | Le Hangar à Bananes | tel. 02 40 47 68 45 | Budget*

LA CIGALE

Charming Art Nouveau style listed traditional brasserie. Although the menu offers fish and seafood, the "Cicada" is also a lovely place to go for breakfast. *Daily | 4, Place Graslin | tel. 02 51 84 94 94 | www.lacigale.com | Moderate*

LA CIVELLE

Seafood, salads and massive steaks in an idyllic setting in Trentemoult. *Sept–April closed Sun evening | 21, Quai Marcel Boissard | tel. 02 40 75 46 60 | www.la-civelle. com | Moderate*

INSIDER TIP PICKLES RESTAURANT

An Englishman cooks for the French in his tiny, lovingly designed restaurant – to much acclaim. Dominic Quirke's cuisine is based on regional products and French traditions, but also plays with Asian and Italian influences – although he will also create a four-course menu with the matching beers. *Sun/Mon, Tue evening and Sat lunchtime closed. | 2, Rue du Marais | tel. 02 51 84 11 89 | www.pickles-restaurant.com | Moderate*

INSIDER TIP LE SQUARE

Creative interpretations of French classics are served in this chic restaurant near the Cité des Congrès. Try the oysters in seaweed butter! *Closed Sun | 14, Rue Jemappes | tel. 02 40 35 98 09 | www. lesquare-nantes.fr | Budget–Moderate*

SHOPPING

The main shopping street is the pedestrian zone, *Rue Crébillon*. The 19th century *Passage Pommeraye (Rue de la Fosse)*, which has wooden floors and cast-iron balustrades, is well worth a visit. *Debotté Maître Chocolatier (9, Rue de la Fosse, and 15, Rue Crébillon)* sells *mascarons nantais*, heavenly chocolates with croquant. Every bit as good: *Les Rigolettes Nantaises (18, Rue de Verdun)*. Be sure to try *nez grillés* as well, which are made of caramel, salted butter and chocolate! The *market at Talensac (Tue–Sun | Rue de Talensac | tram no. 2 and buses 12, 32, 52)* sells vegetables, fish, furniture and clothing. And the bakery *La Petite Boulangerie* and ● *Fromagerie Beillevaire* are two of the top destinations in their fields. Lovingly made paper and writing tools are available from *Papeterie Les P'tits Papiers (2, Place Félix Fournier)*. Pretty children's clothes can be purchased from *Million Dollar Baby (17, Rue du Château)*, and gifts for babies and parents at *Dröm (31, Rue de Verdun)*.

The bar at Le Lieu Unique offers arts and culture instead of cakes and munchies

LEISURE & SPORT

Electric boats for hire for Erdre and Sèvre: *Ruban Vert (Île de Versailles | tel. 02 51 81 04 24 | www.rubanvert.fr)*. Canoe and kayak tours and stand-up paddling on the Sèvre: *Canoë-Kayak Vertou (Blvd. Guichet Serex | Parc de Loisirs du Loiry | tel. 02 40 34 29 97 | www.canoe kayakvertou.com)* in the south-east suburb of Vertou. Night-time canoe trips on the Erdre: *Nack (Route de la Jonelière | La Chapelle-sur-Erdre | tel. 02 40 29 25 71 | www.nack.fr)*

ENTERTAINMENT

There is much praise for the high standard of the opera performances at the *Théâtre Graslin (Place Graslin | tel. 02 40 69 77 18 | www.angers-nantes-ope ra.com)*. A popular meeting place is the *L'Hangar à Bananes (21, Quai des Antilles | www.hangarabananes.com)* on the western end of the Île de Nantes. Where bananas use to be stored for ripening is now home to an art gallery, bars with

views of the Loire and a night club. *Le Lieu Unique (Quai Ferdinand-Favre | www. lelieuunique.com)*, once a biscuit factory, is now the national centre for contemporary art; also has a bar and club.

WHERE TO STAY

INSIDER TIP ▶ BATEAU LE D'Ô

Sleep on the Erdre. This boat with just one room has a chic galley, terrace and oodles of atmosphere. *1 room | 4, Quai Henri Barbusse | tel. 06 99 77 00 20 | sur-prenantes.com | Expensive*

LOFTNANTES

860 ft² apartment for up to six people in the historic shopping gallery Passage Pommeraye – a dream. *no tel. | loft-nantes@gmail.com|www.loftnantes. com | Expensive*

POMMERAYE

You can't get more central than this, located right in the pedestrian precinct. Pleasant rooms without any frills and a breakfast buffet with locally grown produce. *50 rooms | 24, Rue Boileau | tel. 02 40 48 78 79 | www.hotel-pommeraye. com | Budget*

SOZO HOTEL

The very location of this chic boutique hotel in a converted 19th-century chapel makes it unusual. The rooms are fitted with the latest high-tech equipment. *24 rooms | 16, Rue Frédéric Cailliaud | tel. 02 51 82 40 00 | www.sozohotel.fr | Expensive*

INFORMATION

9, Rue des États | tel. 08 92 46 40 44 (*) | www.nantes-tourisme.com | www.levoy ageanantes.fr

PORNIC

(136 B3) *(∅ B4)* ⭐ **The residents of this most important and probably loveliest coastal resort (pop. 14,000) on the Côte de Jade once travelled as far as Newfoundland to catch cod.**

Today, there are only a dozen fishing boats still used but room for 300 yachts in the marina. Romantic writers and artists such as Gustave Flaubert and Auguste Renoir were enchanted by the atmosphere here back in the 19th century. The medieval upper town is on one side of the fishing harbour with the old villa district rising up the other side and along the cliffs. The 14 km/8.7 mi ⩗ *Sentier des Douaniers* follows the cliffs and has beautiful views of Noirmoutier.

FOOD & DRINK

ANNE DE BRETAGNE ⩗

The hotel restaurant 8 km/5 mi to the west in *La-Plaine-sur-Mer* is where chef de cuisine Philippe Vételé, holder of two Michelin stars, creates his culinary wonders. Food, wine and the views of the ocean guarantee an unforgettable – if rather expensive – evening. *Closed Mon and at lunchtime on Tue, Wed | 183, Blvd. la Tara | Port de la Gravette | tel. 02 40 21 54 72 | www.annedebretagne. com | Expensive*

AUBERGE LA FONTAINE AUX BRETONS

Traditional seasonal food in the hotel of the same name. *Daily | Plage de la Fontaine aux Bretons | Chemin des Noëlles | tel. 02 51 74 08 08 | www.auberge-la-fontaine.com | Budget–Moderate*

INSIDER TIP ▶ CRÊPERIE DE LA FRAISERAIE

The menu offers various crêpes and galettes (savoury crêpes) and ice cream specialities. Try the galette with scallops! *Except for July/Aug closed Sun evening and Tuesday | Place du Petit Nice | tel. 02 40 82 39 65 | www.lafraiseraie.com | Budget*

LA POISSONNERIE DU MÔLE

Excellent, imaginatively prepared fish dishes, seafood and meat with Asian accents in the fishing harbour. *closed Mon lunchtime and Wed | Rue de la Marine | tel. 02 40 21 04 86 | www.la-poissonnerie-du-mole.fr | Budget–Moderate*

LA SOURCE ⩗ 🌍

Excellent seafood – buffet on Wed evenings – is served in this restaurant. It enjoys sea views. The focus is on regional produce served with local organic wine. *Daily | Plage de la Source | tel. 02 40 82 21 21 | Moderate*

SHOPPING

⬤ The *market (Place des Halles et de la Terrasse | Thu and Sun 8am–1pm)* is housed in a 17th-century building. An arts and crafts market is also held every Thu evening in summer. To see Breton stoneware being painted by hand, visit the *Faïencerie de Pornic (Rue de la Faïencerie | guided tours Tue and Thu 2.30pm, July/Aug also Wed 3.30pm | www.faience rie-pornic.fr)*.

SPORT & BEACHES

There are five beaches with lifeguards, and the sporting activities range from bike and boat hire, diving, sailing, surfing and rowing to an 18-hole golf course and horse riding.

ENTERTAINMENT

Tropical rum cocktails are served at the Rhumerie *La Casaboubou (Place des Halles)*. Lovely for chilling over oysters and cocktails: *Bernie Café (Port de Plaisance)*. Play roulette and Black Jack at the *casino (www.casinopornic.com)* on the *Quai Leray*.

WHERE TO STAY

ALLIANCE PORNIC RESORT HOTEL THALASSO & SPA

Comfortable hotel with a thalassotherapy centre right on the seafront. *120 rooms | Plage de la Source | tel. 02 40 82 21 21 | www.thalassopornic.com | Expensive*

BEAU SOLEIL

Lovely modern rooms in the best position below the castle in the harbour. *17 rooms | 70, Quai Leray | tel. 02 40 82 34 58 | www.hotel-beausoleil-pornic. com | Moderate*

INSIDER TIP **LES VOLETS BLEUS**
Charming guesthouse in a pretty garden just 200 m /656 ft from the harbour and

Low tide in Pornic harbour

500 m/1640 ft from the beach. *5 rooms | 22, Rue de la Source | tel. 02 40 82 65 99 | www.volets-bleus.net | Budget*

INFORMATION

Place de la Gare | tel. 02 40 82 04 40 | www.ot-pornic.fr

WHERE TO GO

SAINT-BRÉVIN-LES-PINS

(136 B2–3) (*Ø B3*)
The long and very firm sandy beaches of the small, traditional coastal resort just 20 km/12.4 mi north of the Loire estuary are ideal for beach surfers. Also offers all kinds of water sports, plus the *Forêt de la Pierre Attelée* for hiking, and a casino.

CÔTE DE LUMIÈRE

This stretch of coastline is a myriad of light. The Atlantic sparkles and glitters and a hazy shimmer hovers over the marshland in the midday heat. The countryside between Île de Noirmoutier and where the Gironde meets the sea is a wide open landscape with sheer endless expanses of sand at low tide. The smell of salt and the sound of seagulls lie in the air. This section of the coast is the perfect place for a holiday.

With well cared for, lively centres such as La Rochelle, traditional fishing villages and nature reserves as well as fashionable holiday destinations such as the little towns and villages on Ré, this is arguably the most exclusive section of the French Atlantic Coast and one that offers any amount of variety. The some

2200 hours of sunshine annually, 250 km/155 mi of coast – with 140 km/87 mi of sandy beaches – and unpolluted water are additional plus points. And you can buy oysters on virtually every street corner as you can buy sandwiches elsewhere. The Vendée is the most visited holiday region in France after the départements of Var and the Côte d'Azur. But, although tourism is the most important source of income virtually everywhere, agriculture and salt farming are very much part of everyday life here too.

ÎLE D'OLÉRON

(138 B3–4) *(₥ C–D8)* **The island of ★ Oléron (pop. 22,000) is 30 km/18.6 mi**

Sun, salt and sea: 2200 hours of sunshine a year and the snow-white salt ponds have given the 'Coast of Light' its name

long and 15 km/9.3 mi at its widest point. It still exudes its traditional charm, being a little more rustic than Ré.

Oyster farming, brightly-coloured markets, little harbours, towering hollyhocks in cottage gardens – this is where you can relax in a rural setting. Salt marshes, two forested areas, vineyards in the north towards the cliffs on the headland and, not least of all, 100 km/62 mi of cycle paths offer something for everyone. The west coast is ideal for surfers, the sheltered east coast for children and less experienced watersports enthusiasts. The 3 km/1.9 mi-long bridge to the mainland, built in 1966, is toll free. Oyster farming is the most important source of income after tourism.

WHERE TO GO ON OLÉRON

BOYARDVILLE

This pretty village on the east coast has a fishing port and marina, good shops and restaurants and a vast sandy beach. *Fort Boyard* was built offshore by Napoleon in the 19th century on an outcrop of rock and sand to defend the mouth of the Charente. It sits in the water like perfectly circular pebble and can be viewed from the outside only – boat trips available

INSIDER TIP *Les Jardins d'Aliénor (8 rooms | 7 and 11, Rue de Maréchal Foch | tel. 05 46 76 48 30 | www.lesjardinsdalienor.com | Expensive)* is a comfortable and beautifully furnished

Oyster huts were turned into varied ateliers in Le Château-d'Oléron

from Boyardville. The wooded area, the *Forêt des Saumonards*, starts to the north of the village.

LE CHÂTEAU-D'OLÉRON

The first village you come to on the island is so delightful that you might not want to go any further! The largest *market* on the island takes place on Sunday mornings on the *Place de la République*. The *citadelle* offers lovely views of the mainland. **INSIDER TIP** *Artists' studios (www.couleurs-cabnes.fr)* occupy the around 20 little brightly-coloured wooden huts in the fishing port below. These were previously used for oyster farming until EU legislation forced them to move into 'proper' buildings. Now you can watch painters and potters at work and of course buy their wares.

hotel with a very good restaurant *(Sept–June closed Tue lunchtime and Mon)*. Information: *Place de la République | tel. 05 46 47 60 51 | www.ot-chateau-oleron.fr*

LA COTINIÈRE

250 fishermen still go about their business here making La Cotinière less a picturesque harbour and more a bustling fishing port. Fish for dinner can be bought in the *Marché de Victorine* right on the harbour. The restaurant *L'Écailler (daily | 65, Rue du Port | tel. 05 46 47 10 31 | www.ecailler-oleron.com | Moderate)* serves delicious seafood with a view of the harbour. You can also eat in *La Marine* bar *(61, Rue du Port)* which is where the party crowd meet until all hours of the night.

LE GRAND-VILLAGE-PLAGE

The place gets its name from the 15 km/9.3 mi-long beach – a paradise for sun-worshippers and watersports enthusiasts. In Le Petit Village there is a salt harbour and the *Écomusée du Port-des-Salines (July/Aug Mon–Sat 10am–7pm, Sun 2pm–7pm, April–June and Sept Mon/ Tue and Thu–Sat 10am–12.30pm and 2pm–6pm, Wed 10am–6pm, Sun 2pm–6pm | www.oleron-nature-culture.com)*, that gives an insight into the secrets of salt and oyster farming. There are also boats for hire and a market where oysters can be sampled. The restaurant ● Le Relais des Salines *(daily | Port des Salines | tel. 05 46 75 82 42 | www.lere laisdessa lines.com | Moderate)*, located in a row of little oyster farm huts, is famous for its seafood. Information: *3, Blvd. de la Plage | tel. 05 46 47 58 00 | www.legrandvillageplage.fr*

SAINT-DENIS-DE-OLÉRON

The northernmost place on the island (pop. 1200) has a large sailing harbour, a church with a charming portal, and a tower from the 14th century. Also worth seeing are the 46 m/151 ft high ⚡ lighthouse *Phare de Chassiron (daily guided tours, July/Aug also in the late evening | tel. 05 46 76 80 56 or email visites@chas-siron.net to book)* on the northern tip of Olérons, the Pointe de Chassiron. Brightly coloured mobile homes can be rented on the *Camping Le Chassiron (17, Rue des Pérots | tel. 05 46 76 80 56 | camping-lechassiron.blogspot.de | Budget)* at the foot of the lighthouse. Information: *2, Blvd. d'Antioche | tel. 05 46 47 95 53 | www.saintdenisoleron.fr*

SAINT-GEORGES-D'OLÉRON

The largest village on the island (pop. 3350) is in the north near a 15 km/9.3 mi-long beach with lots of campsites. To the

south, its adjoins the *Forêt Domaniale de Domino*. At the centre of the village is the Romanesque *church* (11th/12th century) with a richly decorated façade. In summer, the *market hall* dating from the 19th century is a popular meeting place.

The pleasant *Hotel L'Hermitage (34 rooms | 198, Route de l'Hermitage | tel. 05 46 76 52 56 | www.lhermitage-oleron.com | Moderate)* is 800 m/2624 ft from the beach Les Sables Vignier. It boasts a heated outdoor pool, restaurant and friendly service. The campsite *La Caravane Oléronaise | tel. 05 46 76 52 31 | www.camp ingsablesvignierplage.com* can be recommended. It has 33 pitches, a restaurant and pool and is also close to Les Sables Vigniers. Information: *28, Rue des Dames | tel. 05 46 76 63 75 | www.saint-georges-oleron.com*

SAINT-PIERRE-D'OLÉRON
The capital of the island (pop. 6600) is surrounded by supermarkets but has a pretty town centre with lots of shops and places to go. A market is held on the last Tue of every month on the huge *Place Gambetta* which otherwise doubles as a free car park. Concerts from blues to salsa are held here in the summer. The interactive *Musée de l'Île d'Oléron (April–June and Sept/Oct daily 10am–noon and 2pm–6pm, July/Aug 10am–7pm, Nov–March Tue–Sun 2pm–6pm)* that documents the island's history is also on this square. A roofed *market* operates every day in summer and during the school holidays, as well as on Tue, Thu, Sat and Sun in the low season, on Place Camille Mémain.

The 17th-century *church* with its light-coloured, 43 m/141.1 ft tower that used to help ships navigate, and the *Lanterne des Morts* – the 'lantern of the Dead' – a 23.5 m/77 ft tower from the 12th century, are among the sights worth seeing. There is also a *botanical garden (La Boirie | April–Oct Mon–Sat 10am–noon and 3pm–6pm, Sun 3pm–6pm | www.lesjar dinsdelaboirie.com)* with plants from all over the world. The *Maison des Aïeules (13, Rue Pierre Loti)*, which is not open to visitors, was the home of the writer Pierre Loti (1850–1923). Even as a child he used to spend the holidays here with his parents, and later on the house was a source of inspiration to him. His final resting place is in the garden.

The 9-hole *Golf d'Oléron (Chemin de la Prade | tel. 05 46 47 11 59 | www.golfy.fr)* is on the coast to the east of the town. There's dancing all year round at *Le Bus Stop (Tue–Sat | 1bis, Rue d'Aliénor d'Aquitaine | www.lebusstop.fr).* As well as excellent cocktails. Information: *Place Gambetta | tel. 05 46 85 65 23 | www. saint-pierre-oleron-tourisme.fr*

ÎLE DE RÉ

(130 A–B2) (*∅ C–D7*) The toll to cross the almost 3 km/1.9 mi-long bridge to the ★ Île de Ré (pop. 18,000) costs 16 euros during the high season. Not very welcoming – but it's not supposed to be either.

Ever since the bridge was completed in 1988, the islanders have been torn between the luxury of being able to drive to La Rochelle in less than 20 minutes and the fear that their island could be inundated by many too many day-trippers. It was discussed at length as to whether to abolish the toll or not and just keep the environmental charge of a little more than 3 euros. However, the fear of too many visitors finally won the day. The toll is still 16 euros in the main season and 8 euros for the rest of the year (return) – and is still hotly debated on the island, which has 110 km/68 mi of cycle paths (often idyllic and far from the traffic; bikes can be hired in all the towns), long sandy beaches and very expensive holiday resorts. So it has everything for a very active (if not necessarily inexpensive) beach holiday.

On the north coast there are a number of villages and harbours and an almost 15 km/9.3 mi-long beach down the Atlantic coast. The most beautiful beaches are *Plage de la Conche* and *Plage du Marchais* in the northwest corner. Surfing is one of the most popular pastimes on the island. There are more than enough opportunities to either watch others falling into the water or to risk going out on a board yourself. The surfing hotspots are *Plage de Lizay* near Les-Portes-en-Ré, *La Pergola* in La-Couarde, the south beach in *Rivedoux-Plage*, *Les Grenettes* and *Pas des Biettes* in Sainte Marie and *Gros Jonc* in Le Bois-Plage.

Île de Ré, however, also has a traditional side. As in Guérande and on Noirmoutier and Oléron, salt is also harvested on Ré. The island's countryside is largely unspoilt. More than 300 species of bird have been counted in the sanctuary near Ars.

Hollyhocks and the eye-catching clock tower of Ars: the unmistakeable Île de Ré

WHERE TO GO ON RÉ

ARS-EN-RÉ

The prominent black-and-white church tower in this village (pop. 1300) can be seen from a long way away, rising above the salt marshes like a navigation mark for ships – which in fact is what it really is used for. Well-kept narrow streets lead to a selection of good shops and restaurants.

A visit to the harbour, the island's main sailing harbour, is worth it just for the excellent Breton *galettes* at the **INSIDER TIP** *Café du Commerce (daily | 6, Quai Prée | tel. 05 46 29 41 57 | www.cafcom-ars. com | Budget)*, and to see the decorations, which are from all over the world and range from masks to golf clubs to engravings of old ships. The elegant but uncluttered atmosphere and excellent regional specialities – fish and seafood as well as potatoes from the island – make *Ô de Mer Bistrot Gourmand (closed Sun evening, Tue midday and Mon | 5, Rue Thiers | tel. 05 46 29 23 33 | www.odemer bistrotgourmand.fr | Expensive)* a good choice. The hotel *Thalacap (89 rooms | Av. d'Antioche | tel. 05 46 29 10 00 | www.*

cote-thalasso.fr | Expensive) has its own thalassotherapy centre. Information: *26, Place Carnot | tel. 05 46 29 46 09 | www.iledere-arsenre.com*

LE BOIS-PLAGE-EN-RÉ

This almost 15 km/9.3 mi-long beach in the south of the island is a real holiday paradise. To the west is the pretty village *La Couarde-sur-Mer,* followed by *Bois,* with Sainte-Marie-de-Ré to the southeast. Le Bois-Plage, the largest settlement on the south coast, is surrounded by woods and vineyards. Ré grapes are made into wine, Cognac and Pineau. The beach is particularly suitable for children as there are no sudden drops. You can swim regardless of the tides. Several companies rent out catamarans, surfboards and kayaks and give sailing lessons, e.g. *École de Voile du Bois-Plage La Cabane Verte (tel. 05 46 09 94 73 | www.lacabaneverte.com)* on the Plage de Gros Jonc; surfing and windsurfing at *Ré Surf (Plage de Gros Jonc | tel. 06 30 08 12 81 | www.re-surf.com).*

sive) is stylishly but unostentatiously furnished. It boasts a pool, a spa, a lovely garden and a restaurant. Information: *87, Rue des Barjottes | tel. 05 46 09 23 26 | www.leboisplageenre-tourisme.com*

LA FLOTTE

An idyllic holiday resort with up-market shops and restaurants around a pretty harbour. Boutiques and hairdressers

At La Martinière, you'll find *tout* Saint-Martin queueing. Try the salted caramel ice cream!

The hotel *Les Gollandières (32 rooms | Av. Les Gollandières | tel. 05 46 09 23 99 | www.lesgollandieres.com | Expensive)*, with a pool and restaurant, is situated just behind the dunes on *Plage des Gollandières*. The hotel and holiday apartment complex *Jerodel (12 rooms | 35, Rue de la Glacière | tel. 05 46 09 96 42 | www.jerodel.com | Expensive)* has a heated pool and is just a short distance out of the village but also close to the beach. The hotel *L'Océan (30 rooms | 172, Rue Saint-Martin | tel. 05 46 09 23 07 | www.re-hotel-ocean.com | Moderate–Expen-*

jostle for space on the Rue Général-de-Gaulle. A *market* is held every morning in summer on the Place du Vieux-Marché. Fish specialities at the restaurant ✳ *L'Écailler (closed Mon, Sept–June also Tue | 3, Quai de Sénac | tel. 05 46 09 56 40 | www.lecailler-iledere.com | Expensive)* can be enjoyed with a lovely view of the harbour. The very exlusive *Hôtel Le Richelieu (29 rooms | 44, Av. de la Plage | tel. 05 46 09 60 70 | www.hotel-le-richelieu.com | Expensive)* on the beach has its own thalassotherapy centre. *Le Français (33 rooms | 1, Cours Félix*

Faure | tel. 05 46 09 60 06 | www.hotel
lefrancais.com | *Moderate*), located on
the harbour with its own restaurant, is
more down-to-earth.

SAINT-MARTIN-DE-RÉ

The island's glamourous little capital
(pop. 2600), with its marina, chic bars
and restaurants and elegant hotels, is
like Saint-Tropez's twin town on the Atlantic. This is the liveliest place on the island, especially in the evening. The town
is encircled by ramparts that have been
declared a Unesco World Heritiage Site.
Cars must be parked outside (free of
charge). The ⚴ *church tower* offers lovely views of the town. Choose a seat at
one of the cafés and watch the comings
and goings on the streets and in the harbour that drains completely at low tide!
While strolling around the picturesque
harbour, a visit to the ice cream parlour
*La Martinière (daily | 17, Quai de la
Poithevinière | la-martiniere.fr)* is well
worth while: try the caramel or
INSIDER TIP *fleur de sel* ice cream. Fish
and seafood are to be found in *Le Belem
(daily | 29, Quai de la Poithevinière | tel.
05 46 09 56 56 | Moderate)* and regional
cuisine in *Le Bistrot du Marin (closed Thu |
10, Quai Nicolas Baudin | tel. 05 46
68 74 66 | www.bistrotdumarin.com |
Moderate)* on the island in the harbour.
The dignified and elegant *Hôtel de Toiras*
on the old harbour *(20 rooms | 1, Quai
Job Foran | tel. 05 46 35 40 32 | www.ho-
tel-de-toiras.com | Expensive)* has a 17th-
century façade and a pretty garden. The
*Hôtel Les Colonnes (27 rooms | 19, Quai
Job Foran | tel. 05 46 09 21 58 | www.ho-
tellescolonnes.com | Moderate)* with love-
ly ⚴ rooms, some of which have delightful views of the sea and the marina,
lies in the middle of the island in the harbour. The organisation *Pierre et Vacances
(Rue des Gouverneurs | www.pierreetva*

cances.com) has holiday flats in club-like
complexes. Information: *2, Av. Victor
Bouthillier | tel. 05 46 09 20 06 | www.
saint-martin-de-re.net*

LA ROCHELLE

▓▓ **MAP INSIDE BACK COVER**
▓▓ (138 B2–3) *(ﾑ D7)* **La Rochelle
(pop. 74,000) is a small metropolis that
hosts an international film festival, the
Francofolies music festival in July and has
a university, which was founded in 1993.**
The yacht harbour Les Minimes is the biggest one on Europe's Atlantic coast, and
gives La Rochelle a distinctly southern flair.
The picturesque ★ *old town*, which is hidden behind the old harbour and a façade
front full of cafés, creates an atmosphere
of relaxed busy-ness with its shops and
restaurants. The arcades that stretch for
almost 3 km/1.9 mi make shopping in the
rain a pleasure. But make sure you look up
too – lots of the façades are decorated
with gargoyles and carved stone heads.
Just like Nantes and Bordeaux, the town
benefitted from trade between Europe,
West Africa and the Caribbean. The vineyards and salt ponds also contributed to
its wealth, as did the port of course. This
remained unchanged until the Siege of La
Rochelle during the Wars of Religion in the
17th century when the town was a Protestant stronghold. After 13 months, only
5400 of the 28,000 inhabitants were still
alive; the town was stripped of all its priv-
ileges and rights and it was to be 300
years before it would flourish again as it
had done before.
La Rochelle is easy to explore by bike, not
just because of the many bike paths, but
also because of the ⚫ INSIDER TIP *yellow
bikes*, which are available on the Place de
Verdun and the Place de la Motte Rouge
from the Office de Tourisme for a deposit

(first half-hour free, then 1 euro for every hour; long-term hires are much cheaper). The road surfaces may not always be ideal but they have a lot of stories to tell. The bumpy cobbles in the shipowners' district around Rue Nicolas Venette come from the Saint Lawrence River in Canada – a reminder of trading times with Quebec, a city that was founded by a native of La Rochelle in 1608.

La Rochelle is up-to-date in its inevironmental policy, and not just for its free yellow bikes. The town's progressive traffic concept includes the ⚡ *Libre Service Véhicule Électrique (information from the tourist office)*, which has electric cars at 13 stations that can be hired for 10 euros an hour (cheaper by subscription).

SIGHTSEEING

AQUARIUM ●
10,000 different species, including 20 different types of shark, all swimming above the visitors' heads, and a pool of piranhas in the Amazon greenhouse: these underwater worlds are unbelievably fascinating! *Bassin des Grands Yachts | April–Sept daily 9am–8pm (July/Aug 9am–11pm), Oct–March 10am–8pm | www.aquarium-larochelle.com*

HÔTEL DE VILLE
The lovely town hall, which resembles a knight's castle, overlooks the Place de l'Hôtel de Ville to the cafés La Poste and La Renaissance. For 700 years it has been the official seat of the first citizen of the town. Two-thirds of it were destroyed in a major fire in 2013, although the refurbishment of the building, which boasts towers and battlements, is due to be completed in 2019.

MUSÉE DES BEAUX ARTS
European paintings from the 15th–20th centuries in a Neo-Classicist *palais. 28, Rue Gargoulleau | July–Sept Mon and Wed–Fri 10am–1pm and 1.45pm–6pm, Sat/Sun 2pm–6pm, Oct–June Mon and Wed–Fri 9.30am–12.30pm and 1.45pm–5pm, Sat/Sun 2pm–6pm*

MUSÉE DU FLACON À PARFUM
This small museum has a collection of more than 1000 unusual perfume bottles and powder boxes. *33, Rue du Temple | July/Aug Mon–Sat 10.30am–7pm, Sept–June Tue–Sat 2.30pm–7pm*

MUSÉE MARITIME
Experience the lives of meteorologists and fishermen at sea on the meteorological ship "France I" and seven other historic vessels. The France I has the pleasant INSIDER TIP *Bar du France I*, which is open until the small hours. *Bassin des Chalutiers | April–Sept daily 10am–6.30pm (July/Aug 7pm) | www.musee maritimelarochelle.fr*

MUSÉE DU NOUVEAU MONDE
In La Rochelle, the New World generally means Canada. The exhibition in a

WHERE TO START?
The **Vieux Port** is the place to start any visit. From here, the most important sights in the Old Town and port can all be reached easily on foot or on one of the yellow rental bikes. A lovely way to reach the town centre is on a *bus de mer* from the free car park Les Minimes. The car parks Bernard Loitessier at the Musée Maritime, Rieupeyrot next to the Technoforum and the Esplanade des Parcs in the centre are also free. For those arriving by train, lines 41 and 43 go to Place du Verdun.

magnificent patrician's house traces the links between France and America with colonial furniture, paintings, documents, etc. *10, Rue Fleuriau | July–Sept*

TOWERS 🌿

The 14th-century *Tour de la Chaîne* and *Tour Saint-Nicolas* once guarded the port and testify to the wealth and ex-

Imposing towers guard the entrance to the Vieux Port in La Rochelle

Mon and Wed–Fri 10am–12.30pm and 1.45pm–6pm, Sat/Sun 2pm–6pm, Oct–June Mon and Wed–Fri 9.30am–12.30pm and 1.45pm–5pm, Sat/Sun 2pm–6pm

SAINT-SAUVEUR

The to-ings and fro-ings of the Wars of Religion can be traced in this church on the harbour. The tower dates from the 15th century, the nave was rebuilt in the 17th century after the Catholics were expelled in the 16th century and all Catholic churches in La Rochelle were demolished. The stones were used for the town's fortifications. Only the church towers were left – as watchtowers and platforms for canons.

After the Counter Reformation everything changed once again. At the present day, there are only a few Protestant churches here.

tent of the town that had to be defended. The 70 m/229.9 ft-high *Tour de la Lanterne* was once a lighthouse and a prison for a time, as testified by the graffiti. *Daily 10am–1pm and 2.15pm–5.30pm, April–Sept until 6.30pm | www.tours-la-rochelle.fr*

FOOD & DRINK

ANDRÉ

Fish and seafood at the foot of the two towers on the Old Port. *Daily | 5, Rue Saint-Jean du Pérot | tel. 05 46 41 28 24 | www.barandre.com | Moderate*

CHRISTOPHER COUTANCEAU 🌿

Christopher Coutanceau's cuisine holds two Michelin stars – as did that of his father Richard before him. The excellent food is matched by the heavenly

LA ROCHELLE

views of the ocean. *closed Sun/ Mon/ Plage de la Concurrence | tel. 05 46 41 48 19 | www.coutanceaula rochelle.com | Expensive*

L'ENTRACTE

Chic bistro with very high culinary standards. The menu contains modern interpretations of French classics. The delights include *foie gras* with raspberry crisps. *daily | 35, Rue Saint-Jean-du-Pérot | tel. 05 46 52 26 69 | www.lentracte.net | Moderate*

CAFÉ DE LA PAIX

Pretty Art Nouveau café and bistro with a high varied menu offering everything from salads to mussels and fish. The writer Georges Simenon was a regular here. *closed Sun/ 54, Rue Chaudrier | tel. 05 46 41 39 79 | Budget*

SHOPPING

Rue des Merciers, Rue du Palais and *Rue Chaudrier* are good addresses for clothes, accessories and culinary souvenirs – for which the *market hall (daily in the morning | Place du Marché)* is well worth a visit. The ★ *Grand Marché* is held on Wed and Sat. The market is actually so big that as well as the market hall, the entire surrounding quarter, the *Quartier du Marché*, becomes a market with stalls selling flowers, cheese, fruit and clothing. Regional specialities include cognac, Pineau des Charentes and the goat's cream cheesecake *tourteau fromager*. A fabulous experience for looking around, shopping and taking photos!

SPORTS & ACTIVITIES

Sailing – *École de Voile Rochelaise (Av. de la Capitainerie | tel. 05 46 44 49 20 | www. voile-rochelaise.com)* – and boating –

Aunis Motonautic | Les Minimes | tel. 05 46 44 23 66 | www.aunismotonautic.fr) – are all part of any maritime experience.

ENTERTAINMENT

The nicest way to spend an evening is to drift from one café to the next around the harbour. Later on you can head for the clubs *Oxford Club (Promenade de la Concurrence | www.oxford-club.fr)* and *Le Triolet (8, Rue des Carmes | letrioletclub.com).*

WHERE TO STAY

BEST WESTERN CHAMPLAIN FRANCE ANGLETERRE

Grand villa right next to Place de Verdun with a large garden for breakfast and to relax in, and very spacious rooms. *36 rooms | 30, Rue Rambaud | tel. 05 46 41 23 99 | www.hotelchamplain.com | Moderate*

RÉSIDENCE DE FRANCE

The primary hotel on the square, also close to the Place de Verdun, offers every imaginable comfort, including a heated outdoor pool and its own underground garage. There are fabulous views of the old town from the ⚜ top floors. *54 rooms and suites | 43, Rue du Minage | tel. 05 46 28 06 00 | www.hotel-larochelle.com | Expensive*

HÔTEL SAINT NICOLAS

Pleasant hotel on a small square near the fishing port. *86 rooms | 13, Rue Sardinerie | tel. 05 46 41 71 55 | www.hotel-saint-nicolas.com | Moderate*

INFORMATION

2, Quai Georges Simenon | tel. 05 46 41 14 68 | www.larochelle-tour isme.com

WHERE TO GO

CHÂTELAILLON-PLAGE
(138 B–C3) (*⚏ D7*)

This seaside resort (pop. 5900) is 12 km/ 7.5 mi to the south on a 3 km/1.9 mi- long fine sandy beach where wind and kitesurfers congregate at high tide. The villas dating from the Belle Époque and a natural paradise – the perfect backdrop for a quiet day by the sea or an extended exploration of the island on a rented bike (*tel. 05 46 84 58 23 | www.cyclaix.com*). The *Musée Napoléonien (April–Sept daily, Oct Wed–Mon 9.30am–12.30pm and 2pm–6pm, Nov–March Wed–Mon 9.30am–12.30pm and 2pm–5pm)* traces the final three days Bonaparte spent on

La Rochelle's charming old town is just past the old harbour

the ⚏ promenade lined with tamarisk trees with a view of the islands Aix and Oléron, are real plus points. There is also a casino with an adjoining night- club. Information: *5, Av. de Strasbourg | tel. 05 46 56 26 97 | www.chatelaillon- plage-tourisme.fr*

ÎLE D'AIX (138 B3) (*⚏ D8*)

20 km/12.4 mi to the south of La Ro- chelle is the ferry port Fouras. In just 30 minutes by boat from here you can reach the traffic-free Île d'Aix (pop. 200). A vil- lage enclosed within the walls of the Fort de la Rade awaits visitors, surrounded by

French soil in July 1815 on Aix, before be- ing exiled to St Helena. His death mask, several letters – including his unsuccess- ful appeal for asylum in England – as well as his bedroom are on show. In the affiliated *Musée Afrique (April–Sept dai- ly, Oct Wed–Mon 9.30am–12.30pm and 2pm–6pm, Nov–March Wed–Mon 9.30am–12.30pm and 2pm–5pm)* oppo- site, a stuffed camel that Napoleon sup- posedly rode during his campaign in Egypt can be seen as well as a variety of big game and African works of art. Infor- mation: *6, Rue Gourgaud | tel. 05 46 83 01 82 | www.iledaix.fr*

ÎLE DE NOIRMOUTIER ★
(136 A–B4) (*A–B4*)

Salt ponds, oyster beds, fishing harbours, sailing boats and white houses adorned with flowering hibiscus characterise this island (pop. 9600) that is a good 20 km/ 12.4 mi long. The island can be reached via a toll-free bridge 180 km/112 mi from La Rochelle and 70 km/43 mi from Nantes or across a 4 km/2.5 mi-long paved causeway that can be crossed at

The charming focal point of island life is the main town *Noirmoutier-en-l'Île* with shops, restaurants, the Roman-Gothic church *Saint-Philbert* and the well-preserved 12th-century castle. In the castle, the *Musée du Château (Place d'Armes | July/Aug daily 10am–7pm, Feb, April–June and Sept Wed–Mon 10am–12.30pm and 2.30–6pm, Oct, first half Nov and March 2pm–6pm)* explains the island's history. Find out everything you want to know

Island idyll: beach near the forest Bois de la Chaize on Noirmoutier

low tide and disappears at high tide when only the tips of the traffic signs can be seen sticking out of the water. Tourists seldom use this *Passage du Gois*, several cars having been washed away by the incoming tide in the past.

Parts of Noirmoutier, which is an ● ideal place for cycling (rental bikes available in every village) are actually below sea level. Long sandy beaches open up beyond dense pine forests. Nude bathing is also permitted on the *Plage de Luzéronde* on the west coast. There are sailing schools and water sports centres all around the island.

about ship-building at the *Musée de la Construction Navale (Rue de l'Écluse | closed for conversion)*, everything about fishing and salt extraction at the ● *Musée des Traditions de l'Île (Place de l'Église | July/Aug daily 10am–12.30pm and 3pm– 7pm, April–June and Sept–mid Oct Tue– Sat 10am–12.30pm and 2.30pm–6pm)* 5 km/3.1 mi south in *La Guérinière*. Noirmoutier-en-l'Île is located 2 km/1.2 mi from the sea. South of it there is a nature reserve with salt marshes and breeding places. The small elegant hotel INSIDER TIP▶ *Blanc Marine (5 rooms | 1, Rue de l'Acquenette |*

tel. 02 51 39 99 11 | www.blanc-marine. net | *Moderate*) is lovingly managed by Véronique and Jean Dalric who give it a very personal touch. It has a pool and a delightful garden. A very opulent breakfast – by French standards – is included in the price. *Hôtel du Bois de la Chaize (8 rooms | 23, Av. de la Victoire | tel. 02 51 39 04 62 | www.hotel-noirmoutier. com | Moderate)* is a charming small hotel with indoor pool between Plage des Dames and the harbour and is especially suitable for families as it has rooms sleeping up to 6. Imaginative interpretations of traditional island dishes can be found in the small restaurant *Le Vélo Noir (closed Sun/Mon, Wed in July/Aug | 13, Rue du Vieil Hôpital | tel. 02 51 35 85 29 | www.levelonoir.fr | Moderate)*. The trendy crowd gathers at *Café Noir (4, Quai Cassard | tel. 02 51 39 00 75)*.

Politicians and celebrities have their villas on the chic *Plage des Dames*, which covers a number of bays behind the Bois de la Chaize. Right at the north-west is the lovely fishing and holiday resort of *L'Herbaudière*. Creative fish dishes are conjured up there by the multiple award-winning chef Alexandre Couillon at the *La Marine (closed Tue/Wed | 5, Rue Marie Lemonnier | tel. 02 51 39 23 09 | www.ale xandrecouillon.com | Expensive)*. Right next door is Couillon's bistro `INSIDER TIP` *La Table d'Élise (closed Tue/Wed and Sun evening, Wed evening in July/Aug | Rue Marie Lemonnier | tel. 02 28 10 68 35 | Moderate)*, where he serves inexpensive samples of his art. Fish and seafood from the waters around Noirmoutier dominate the menu at the brasserie `INSIDER TIP` *La Plage de Jules (daily | Plage des Dames | 30, Av. Georges Clemenceau | tel. 02 51 39 06 87 | www.les prateaux.com | Budget–Moderate)* with the pretty ≈ terrace (ocean views). Breakfast and cocktails are also available.

The villages of *La Bosse, L'Épine* and *Barbâtre* with their narrow alleyways, low white houses and flowering hibiscus are also extremely picturesque. Information: *Rue du Polder | Barbâtre | tel. 02 51 39 80 71 | www.ile-noirmoutier.com*

ÎLE D'YEU (136 A5) (*A5*)

Sandy beaches to the east, the wild Côte Sauvage to the southwest and pine and oak forests make up the Île d'Yeu (pop. 5000). Located 20 km/12.4 mi from the mainland, it covers an area of 9 mi². It can be reached by ferry from Fromentine and Saint-Gilles-Croix-de-Vie *(www.compag nie-yeu-continent.fr, www.compagnieven deenne.com)*.

Pretty *Port-Joinville* on the sheltered east coast is the main settlement on the island. The principle beach is in neighbouring *Ker-Chalon* with another lovely beach in *Plage des Sabias.* Yeu is best explored by bike (available from dozens of rental places). Dolmens and menhirs testify to the island's early settlement. The most famous is the approx. 5000 years old *Dolmen de la Planche à Puare* on the northwest coast.

The hotel *Grand Large (22 rooms | 1, Rue du Courseau | tel. 02 51 58 36 77 | www. hotel-legrandlarge.fr | Budget)* is right on the harbour in Port-Joinville. Seven charming chambres d'hôtes and two holiday apartments are available to rent from Monsieur et Madame Groisard on the island: at *La Citadelle (49, Rue Saint-Hilaire | tel. 02 51 58 42 30 | Budget)* and in *Port-Joinville (11, Rue Pierre Henry | Port-Joinville | tel. 02 51 58 55 24 | www. yeu-sejour.com | Budget)*. Information: *1, Rue du Marché | tel. 02 51 58 32 58 | www.ile-yeu.fr*

MARAIS POITEVIN ★ ● ≈
(138 B–C 1–2) (*D–E 6–7*)

This extensive marshland area *(www.*

marais-poitevin.com) lies 30 km/18.6 mi to the northeast of La Rochelle. It is criss-crossed by thousands of canals. Since time immemorial, the people here have used flat, black boats as a means of transport – whether it is to go to church or the baker's. Tourists today can do just the same – with a guide, as the network of waterways is one huge labyrinth for the uninitiated. But what a beautiful one! Poplars, willows, ash and tall reeds line the banks watched over by herons. With a little luck, you might even spot some beavers. The starting points include *Arçais, Coulon, Damvix* and *Maillezais*.

Rural charm in a romantic little castle at the heart of the Marais Poitevin is found at the INSIDER TIP *Château de l'Abbaye* (5 rooms | tel. 02 51 56 17 56 | www.cha teau-moreilles.com | *Expensive*) belonging to the Renard family. It has a heated swimming pool, a spa and an abundance of nature in the surrounding area. In the evenings, guests can dine by candlelight on the terrace.

NOTRE-DAME-DE-MONTS
(136 B4) (*∅ B5*)

The coastal resort (pop. 1500) some 150 km/93 mi north of La Rochelle offers the best conditions for water sports and kayak trips along the canals of the marshes. Interesting: *Le Jardin du Vent* (see chapter "Travel with kids") and the new museum *Biotopia* (50, Av. Abbé Thibaud | July/Aug Mon–Fri 10am–7pm, Sat/Sun 2pm–7pm, April–June and Sept–Nov Mon and Wed–Fri 10am–noon and 2pm–6.30pm, Sat/Sun 2pm–6.30pm, Feb/March Wed–Mon 2pm–6.30 Uhr | www. biotopia.fr), with audio-visual and interactive presentations of the nature of the shores, dunes and forest. There are fabulous views of the marsh landscape all around and as far as Noirmoutier from the 70 m/229.7 ft water tower ⚓ INSIDER TIP

Kulmino (July/Aug Mon–Fri 10am–7pm, Sat/Sun 2pm–7pm, April–June and Sept Wed–Sun 2pm–6.30pm | www.kulmino.fr) in the water tower. Information: *6, Rue de la Barre | tel. 02 51 58 84 97 | www.notre-dame-de-monts.fr*

ROCHEFORT (138 C3) (*∅ D8*)

A major attraction in Rochefort (pop. 25,000), some 30 km/18.6 mi to the south, is the *Corderie Royale,* the royal rope factory, a 375 m-long, Baroque building with a landscaped garden situated on the river bank. It comprises the *Centre International de la Mer (April–Sept 10am–7pm, Oct–Dec and Feb/March 10am–12.30pm and 2pm–6pm | www.corderie-royale.com)* with an exhibition on the former royal rope manufacture. A reproduction of the historical three-master, *Hermione*, is moored along the bank. Since 1900 the *Pont Transbordeur (closed until 2019 for renovations | www.pont-transbordeur.fr)*, one of only eight floating ferries left in the world, has connected the town with Échillais on the other side of the Charente. Information: *Av. Sadi-Carnot | tel. 05 46 99 08 60 | www.paysrochefortais-tourisme.com, www.rochefort-ocean.com*

LES SABLES-D'OLONNE
(136 C6) (*∅ B–C6*)

This lively resort (pop. 16,000), with its 3 km/1.9 mi-long beach promenade *Le Remblai*, is 80 km/49.7 mi to the north-west of La Rochelle. The *fishing port*, the 11th-century chapel *Prieuré Saint-Nicolas* and the ⚓ *Tour d'Arundel* lighthouse at the entrance to the harbour channel are well worth seeing.

Delicious seafood can be found at *Le Clipper (closed Mon/Tue, July–mid Sept Tue midday and Thu midday | 19 bis, Quai Guiné | tel. 02 51 32 03 61 | www.le-clipper. com | Moderate)* on the harbour. Just

50 m/164 ft from the Grande Plage is the friendly hotel *Arc en Ciel (37 rooms | 13, Rue Chanzy | tel. 02 51 96 92 50 | www. arcencielhotel.com |* Budget–Moderate*).* Information: *1, Promenade Joffre | tel. 02 51 96 85 85 | www.lessablesdolonne-tourisme.com*

SAINT-GILLES-CROIX-DE-VIE
(136 B5) ( *B5*)

Over 200 fishermen head out to sea from the friendly family resort (pop. 7400) 100 km/62 mi (north of La Rochelle to fish for sardine. The little blue wooden cabins where tourists can leave their swimming things are a feature of the long beach that grows considerably at low tide. If you want even more room to yourselves, head for *Grande Plage* further to the right which stretches along a strip of land between the sea and the mouth of the river Vie. It can only be reached on foot, by bike or water bus (departing from the fishing port). At Port Fidèle in July and August, on Tuesdays (9am–7pm) there is an *artisans' market*, and every evening a *night market*. The *Moulerie de la Gare (closed Mon from Sept–May | 52, Quai de la République | tel. 02 51 55 07 28 |* Budget*)* serves over 50 mussel dishes. Information: *Place de la Gare | tel. 02 51 55 03 66 | www.payssaintgilles-tourisme.fr*

The coast around neighbouring *Saint-Hilaire-de-Riez* is steeper and more rugged. Further north is *Saint-Jean-de-Monts*, famous for its wide sandy beach but lined by hotel complexes and blocks of flats.

LA TRANCHE-SUR-MER
(136 B2) ( *C6*)

13 km/8.1 mi of fine sandy beach and some 250 days of sunshine a year have turned this village (pop. 2700) with its whitewashed cottages, 40 km/24.9 mi north of La Rochelle, into a miniature paradise for sun-worshippers and water-sports enthusiasts. Families with children will find any amount of things to do here too. Information: *Place de la Liberté | tel. 02 51 30 33 96 | www.ot-latranchesurmer.fr*

Pure relaxation: the boatsman will steer you under the willows and through the Marais Poitevin

ROYAN

(138 C5) (𝛺 D9) The roofed market looks like a huge umbrella and its bustling promenade, packed with bars, boutiques and restaurants, curves around the marina of Royan like two outstretched arms.

This town (pop. 18,000), located on the northern bank of the Gironde estuary around a 2 km/1.2 mi-wide bay, has little in common with other resorts in the area apart from its long beach. In the 19th and early 20th century, the moneyed from Bordeaux and writers and artists came here. Émile Zola took photos of the coast and Picasso painted the Café des Bains. That nothing remains of the old town of Royan except for pictures and memories is due to the German army, which engaged in heavy battles with the Allied Forces in January 1945. 85% of the town was destroyed. The reconstruction, inspired by the buildings of the German-Brazilian architect Oscar Niemeyer, has given Royan a touch of tropical architecture. One example is the reinforced concrete church *Notre-Dame*, in which the height of the aisle varies (28–36 m/91.9–118.1 ft). The almost endless, three-storey complex of the *Front de Mer* with restaurants and shops winds its way around the bay in the shape of a broad, rounded line. At the time of its construction, this generous ocean front was the very epitome of modern urban living.

SIGHTSEEING

PLANET EXOTICA ●

The former botanic garden of Royan has outgrown itself. A bonsai collection in the Japanese garden, exotic plants and reptiles in the the orchid and tropical house, and a Jurassic Garden with around 50 life-size models of dinosaurs are just some of the highlights. *5, Av. des Fleurs de la Paix | Easter–Oct. Daily 10am–6pm, June–Aug until 8pm | www.planet-exotica.com*

FOOD & DRINK

INSIDER TIP▶ LES FILETS BLEUS

Fabulous cooking behind an unassuming façade: traditional cuisine with the focus on fish and seafood in an ambience where the colour blue rules. *Closed Sun/Mon | 14, Rue Notre-Dame | tel. 05 46 05 74 00 | Moderate*

SPORTS & BEACHES

Royan's main beach is the 2 km/1.2 mi *Grande Conche* where you can go sailing, kayaking, kitesurfing, surfing and diving. Boat trips available to Ré, Oléron and Aix.

WHERE TO STAY

BEAU RIVAGE ⚓

At one end of the bay with a view of the

Got everything you need? Plenty of luggage for a long day on the beach at the foot of the Phare de la Coubre

sea and the estuary. *22 rooms | 9, Façade de Foncillon | tel. 05 46 39 43 10 | www. hotel-beau-rivage-royan.com | Budget–Moderate*

INFORMATION

1, Blvd. de la Grandière | tel. 05 46 23 00 00 | www.royan-tourisme.com

WHERE TO GO

LA PALMYRE (138 B4) (*D9*)
The resort La Palmyre (pop. 700) lies 17 km/10.6 mi northwest of Royan on the coast surrounded by a pine forest planted in the 19th century covering more than 30 mi². Sandbanks enclose the sheltered bay *Bonne Anse,* that is especially suitable for families. There are also beaches for surfers and a nudist area. La Palmyre is linked to the village *La Tremblade,* that is famous for its oyster farms, by a 35 km/21.8 mi cycle path. The lighthouse, *Phare de la Coubre,* is on the headland nearby. Information: *2, Av. de Royan | tel. 05 46 22 41 07 | www.la-palmyre-les-mathes.com*

PHARE DE CORDOUAN ★ ●
(138 B5) (*D9*)
It used to be possible to walk to the 16th century lighthouse in the Gironde estuary when the tide was out, but today it is 7 km/4.4 mi from the coast and surrounded by waves. It is the oldest still working lighthouse in Europe. You can take a boat trip out to see the 67.5 m/ 219.8 ft tower and climb up the 311 steps. The "Vedette Jules Verne" goes out to the tower from Royan. The trip lasts about four hours, and booking is essential: *Croisières La Sirène (tel. 05 46 05 30 93 | www.croisierelasirene. com). www.phare decordouan.com*

SAINT-PALAIS-SUR-MER
(138 B5) (*D9*)
The distinguishing features of this lively resort (pop. 3400) 6 km/3.7 mi northwest of Royan are its lovely beaches with fine sand, its elegant Belle Époque villas, and the lovely location on the transition between the Gironde estuary and the open ocean. Information: *1, Av. de la République | tel. 05 46 23 22 58 | www.saint-palais-sur-mer.com*

CÔTE D'ARGENT

250 km/155 mi of sandy beach are a good enough argument for a holiday on the Côte d'Argent, the 'Silver Coast'. This strip between the Gironde estuary and the mouth of the Adour near Bayonne owes its name to the glitter of the sun on the sea.

Inland from the coast lies Europe's largest area of forest covering more than 3800 mi². In the early 19th century pines were planted to stop the dunes from drifting further inland and the wetlands were drained.

The lakes a little way in from the coast are an ideal alternative for swimming and watersports to the Atlantic that often shows itself from its untamed side. Many towns and villages are divided into two, with one part on a lake and one on the sea. Europe's highest dune, the Dune du Pilat is particularly impressive, rising to a height of 114–117 m/374–383 ft. It offers a fantastic view of the coast and Arcachon Bay that is perfect for swimming as well as for farming oysters of exceptional quality. Apart from water that gave the Aquitaine region its name, wine also plays an important role. Most wines today are suitably produced in the various famous *châteaux* in Médoc, Haut-Médoc and in the area around Bordeaux.

ARCACHON

(140 A4) (*∅* D12) **This lively resort (pop. 11,000), that is like a big fair-**

Water, woods and wine: endless beaches, powerful breakers and châteaux further inland attract swimmers, surfers and bon vivants

ground at the height of summer, is right on huge Arcachon Bay that covers 60 mi². With is promenade packed with restaurants and the pedestrianised Rue du Maréchal de Lattre de Tassigny with cafés, boutiques and ice cream parlours, it is difficult to believe that the first tourists in Arcachon were those with respiratory problems who came to breathe in the sea air and the smell of the pine trees.

Aristocrats and artists also found the spa fashionable after Napoleon III hol-idayed here in 1863. The 7 km/4.5 mi-long beach and the entertainments for children make this little town ideal for families.

SIGHTSEEING

NOTRE DAME
The INSIDER TIP *Chapelle des Marins*, an 18th-century seaman's chapel, is perhaps more interesting than the 19th-century basilica due to all the votive pictures and buoys that decorate it.

Playful 19th-century architecture: a house in Arcachon's Ville d'Hiver

lous elements. The streets run in rounded arches to outsmart the wind. The resulting protection helps the Mediterranean vegetation to thrive. An overview is provided at the ● ☀ *Observatoire Sainte-Cécile*, an iron construction that Gustave Eiffel helped to create. There are 75 steps up to it.

FOOD & DRINK

CAP PEREIRE
Fish specialities, duck or a steak on a pretty ☀ terrace with views of the Basin of Arcachon. *Closed Sun and Mon evenings | 1, Av. du Parc Pereire | tel. 05 56 83 24 01 | www.restaurantcappereire. com | Moderate*

CHEZ PIERRE
Fish and seafood of very good qualility in the restaurant of *Café de la Plage* near the promenade. *Daily | 1, Blvd. Veyrier-Montagnères | tel. 05 56 22 52 94 | www.cafedelaplage.com | Moderate*

CHEZ YVETTE
An institution in Arcachon, and popular both with visitors and locals. The menu consists mainly of seafood. *Daily | 59, Blvd. du Général Leclerc | tel. 05 56 83 05 11 | www.restaurant-chez-yvette-arcachon.fr | Moderate*

SHOPPING

A *market* is held daily (in winter Tue–Sun) from 7am–1.30pm in the market hall.

SPORTS & BEACHES

The *Plage de Pereire* is 3 km/1.9 mi long and fringed by the promenade. It has play areas, a skate park and lawn areas. The *Plage du Moulleau* is a popular swimming spot with youngsters, while the

VILLE D'ÉTÉ
The 'Summer Town' at the foot of the hill between the pretty station and the promenade along the bank is bursting with life. Boats for Cap Ferret and tours around Arcachon Bay – to Île aux Oiseaux, for example – depart from the main beach. The roulette ball has been spinning in the casino near the beach since 1903.

VILLE D'HIVER ★
The forested "winter town", where the rich and those of poor health from Bordeaux built their residences after the 1870s, is a motley collection of playful architecture, with some foreign and some fabu-

Plage des Arbousiers to the west is a meeting-place for surfers. Surfing, sailing, diving, jet ski, motorboat hire and catamaran tours are offered by various operators in the yacht harbour. Kayak trips and hire are offered by *Arcachon Kayak Adventure (Port de Plaisance, Centre Nautique Pierre Mallet)*, and there is a *Tennis club (7, Av. du Parc | tcarcachon. com)* with 20 sand courts and two halls at the Pereire Park, a footpath that leads all the way around Arcachon Bay and an 18-hole golf course at *Golf International d'Arcachon (35, Blvd. d'Arcachon | tel. 05 56 54 44 00 | www.golfarcachon.org)*. And if you fancy paddling across the bay standing up, then *Surf en Buch (tel. 06 80 05 46 95 | www.ecoledesurf-arcachon. com)* is the right address. The operator also offers INSIDERTIP guided trips for stand-up paddlers, for instance to the oyster banks or along the Dune du Pilat. The dune is the biggest paragliding site in the world. It requires strong nerves and four hours' training, e.g. at the *Waggas School École de Parapente (Pyla-sur-Mer | tel. 06 32 04 32 07 | www.wagga school.com)*.

ENTERTAINMENT

The *Casino d'Arcachon (163, Blvd. de la Plage | www.casinoarcachon.com)* also has a restaurant *(daily)*. There's dancing at the *Metropolitain Club (Thu-Sun 1am–6am | 6, Blvd. Mestrezat)*.

WHERE TO STAY

HÔTEL LES BAINS D'ARGUIN
Elegant spa hotel with thalassotherapy centre, *100 m/328 ft from the beach. 94 rooms | 9, Av. du Parc | tel. 05 57 72 06 72 | www.hotel-bainsdarguin-arcachon. com | Expensive*

HÔTEL DE LA PLAGE
Medium category hotel near the beach with small but bright rooms and friendly service. *55 rooms | 10, Av. Nelly de Deganne | tel. 05 56 83 06 23 | www. hotelarcachon.com | Moderate–Expensive*

⭐ **Dune du Pilat**
The view from the top of Europe's highest dune is an experience not to be missed → p. 68

⭐ **Biscarrosse**
More than just the sea: take a swim in the lake too → p. 68

⭐ **Pauillac**
A 'château crawl' for wine lovers → p. 81

⭐ **Saint-Émilion**
This wine village in the Bordelais has all the charms of France rolled into one → p. 77

⭐ **Courant d'Huchet**
A river and a jungle-like landscape: one of the loveliest areas in the country → p. 80

⭐ **Ville d'Hiver in Arcachon**
The pretty villas in Arcachon's "Winter Town" → p. 66

⭐ **Musée d'Art Contemporain CAPC**
Avant-garde art in an old harbour warehouse in Bordeaux → p. 72

⭐ **La Cité du Vin in Bordeaux**
All about wine in the ultra-modern theme park → p. 72

MARCO POLO HIGHLIGHTS

RESIDHOME APPART HOTEL PLAZZA

Stylish apartment hotel with modern interiors (*89 studios and apartments with kitchens*) 200 m/656 ft from the beach. *49–51, Av. Lamartine | tel. 05 57 15 48 00 | www.residhome.com | Expensive*

GRAND HOTEL RICHELIEU

The old glory of the spa era on the beach. Empress Sissi once stayed here in the 19th century. *45 rooms. | 185, Blvd. de la Plage | tel. 05 56 83 16 50 | www. grand-hotel-richelieu.com | Moderate– Expensive*

INFORMATION

Esplanade Georges Pompidou | tel. 05 57 52 97 97 | www.arcachon-tourisme.com

WHERE TO GO

CAP FERRET
(140 A4) *(∅ D12)*

At the southern tip of the promontory that encloses the Bassin d'Arcachon from the north is the 53 m/173.9 ft high ﹅﹅ *lighthouse (July/Aug daily 10am–7.30pm, April–June and Sept 10am–12.30 and 2–6.30pm, Oct–March Wed–Sun 2pm–7pm)* Fabulous views!

DUNE DU PILAT ★ ● ﹅﹅
(140 A4) *(∅ D12)*

Come before the mass migration that gathers after 10am and perspires its way past the souvenir stands up the 170 steps in the sand to Europe's biggest dune *(114–177 m/374–580 ft high, almost 3 km/1.9 mi long)* 10 km/6.2 mi south of Arcachon. The views of the pine forests, white sandbanks in the deep-blue sea and the dune crests are so fabulous that you shouldn't let the parking fee *(4 euros for up to 4 hours, then 6 euros)* put you off. There are lots

of camp sites right beside the sea south of the dune. Information: *Rond-Point du Figuier/Av. Ermitage | Pyla sur Mer | tel. 05 56 54 53 83 | www.tourisme-latestedebuch.fr*

BISCARROSSE

(140 A5) *(∅ D13)* **A seaside and lake-side resort in one:** ★ **Biscarrosse (pop. 14,000) is divided into three: Plage, Ville and the watersports eldorado Biscarrosse-Lac at the southern end of Lac Nord.**

A cycle path connects the different parts through the slightly hilly countryside. Two canals link Lac Sud, Petit Lac de Biscarrosse and Lac Nord. By connecting the coast with the inland region in such a way, a perfect holiday environment has been created. When the Atlantic is too rough you can head for the northern lake where the gently sloping banks

At the top of the Dune du Pilat between the pine forest and the ocean

are ideal for children too. Watersports enthusiasts have sheer endless possibilities. With its market, boutiques, cafés and 10 km/6.2 mi of beach, Biscarrosse-Plage has all the amenities of a seaside resort.

SIGHTSEEING

MUSÉE DE L'HYDRAVIATION
Seaplanes were designed and tested in Biscarrosse from 1930–55 and their history can be traced in this museum. 332, *Av. Louis Bréguet | Biscarrosse-Ville | July/Aug daily 10am–7pm, Sept–June Tue–Sun 2pm–6pm | hydravions-biscarrosse.com*

FOOD & DRINK

LE BISCANTOU
Down-to-earth regional cuisine in a somewhat sober ambience. *Closed Sat noon, Sun evening and Mon | 49, Place des Chênes Verts | Biscarrosse-Ville | tel. 05 58 78 81 34 | Budget*

INSIDER TIP L'IDYLLE CAFÉ PLAGE
Lovely combination of lounge bar and restaurant on the shore. Bury your feet in the sand (brought in especially) in the tapas bar, while in the restaurant you can enjoy local seafood and wine between breakfast and nightcap – all under the open sky. Occasional concerts in the evening. *Daily | 18, Chemin de Maguide | tel. 05 58 09 87 14 | https://m.facebook.com/idylle.restaurant | Budget*

LE PARCOURS GOURMAND ☆
If you want somewhere a bit smarter: dine in the golf club restaurant with views of the greenery. *Closed Sun evening, Mon evening, Tue evening | Av. du Golf | tel. 05 58 09 84 84 | Moderate*

RESTAUMER
Fish and seafood come directly from the

adjoining poissonnerie – and the atmosphere is as lively and relaxed as you would imagine. *March–Oct daily | 210, Av. de la Plage | tel. 05 58 78 20 26 | www.restaumer.com | Budget*

INSIDER TIP LE SAINT-EX

Traditional cuisine in a charming restaurant named after the writer Antoine de Saint-Exupéry. The author of "The Little Prince" tested seaplanes in Biscarrosse in the 1930s. *Closed Sun evening and Mon evening. | 244, Place Charles de Gaulle | Biscarrosse-Ville | tel. 05 58 78 16 16 | Budget*

SHOPPING

Large *market* with regional products, clothing and souvenirs daily in July and August (on the last two weekends of the month in June, on the first three weekends in September) on the Place Dufau in Biscarrosse-Plage. Also a daily *night market* at the same address.

SPORTS & BEACHES

Sailing, boats for hire, surfing, water-skiingland yachting, boat trips, a beach club for children, diving, golf …: there is virtually nothing that is not available. The southern-most section of the (unmanned) beach is reserved for nudists.

ENTERTAINMENT

The *L'Oceana (46, Rue du Grand Vivier | daily from mid June–Sept, otherwise Fri/Sat)* is a popular club in Biscarrosse-Plage. Concerts and plays are given at *L'Arcanson (61, Av. du Lieutenant de Vaisseau Paris | Biscarrosse-Ville)*. There is also a *Casino (Blvd. des Sables)*.

WHERE TO STAY

CAMPSITES

Biscarrosse has six four-star sites and one five-star site. Waterpark, spa, restaurant, supermarket and more than 800 pitches at *Camping Domaine de la Rive (Route de Bordeaux | tel. 05 58 78 12 33 | www.larive.fr)* on Lac Nord.

LA CARAVELLE ⭐

The only hotel in Biscarrosse-Lac with a view of the lake, beach and moorings. Restaurant with regional cuisine. *11 rooms | 5314, Route des Lacs | tel. 05 58 09 82 67 | www.lacaravelle.fr | Moderate*

INSIDER TIP LE COMPTOIR DES SABLES

Lovely guesthouse with spa 300 m/ 984 ft from the beach. Thoughtfully furnished rooms with a lot of wood and attractively designed bathroom areas, some with private terraces. *5 rooms | 34, Av. de la Libération | Biscarrosse-Plage | tel. 05 58 78 35 20 | www.lecomptoirdessables.fr | Expensive*

INSIDER TIP CÔTE & DUNE

Stylish white wooden building with views of the dunes and its own heated pool and spa. Yoga lessons are also on offer. The five rooms and four apartments are decorated in a bright beach look (and with driftwood items), have a balcony or terrace, and open to the pool. There is a path straight to the beach. *5 rooms | 675, Av. Gabriele D'Annunzio | Biscarrosse-Plage | tel. 05 58 08 17 29 | www.cotedune.fr | Expensive*

LE GRAND HÔTEL DE LA PLAGE ⭐

This stylish, bright white hotel sits high up on a dune with fabulous views of the sea, plus a pool, wellness area and a restaurant with traditional cuisine. *33 rooms | Av. de la Plage | Biscarrosse-Plage | tel. 05 58 82 74 00 | www.legrandhoteldelaplage.fr | Expensive*

INFORMATION

55, Place Georges Dufau | tel. 05 58 78 20 96 | www.biscarrosse.com

BORDEAUX

▓▓ **MAP INSIDE BACK COVER**
▓▓ (140 C3) (*Ⓜ E11*) **Bordeaux, the world capital of wine, capital of the Nouvelle-Aquitaine region and on the Unesco World Heritage List, is not only in an excellent position amongst wine castles and wide beaches, but the city also has its own unique charm.**

Bordeaux received a new landmark in 2013 with the *Pont Jacques Chaban-Delmas*, the biggest lift bridge in Europe with a centre section that can be raised by 50 m/164 ft. The metropolis (pop. 239,000, greater area 660,000) on the Garonne has generally had something of a facelift, as the result of which its architecture is once again seen at its very best. The old town to the south of the vast Esplanade des Quinconces with 5000 classicist listed buildings has been restored, the facades cleaned. Bit by bit, cars are disappearing from the centre. The Old Town has an underground system of tunnels linking the multi-storey car parks; several streets are only open to residents and pedestrians. And if you get tired, take one of the 'green' ⓥ bicycle taxis – rickshaws crisscross the centre along fixed routes.

The city owes it harmonious overall appearance to its remodelling in the 18th century after Bordeaux became rich thanks to the wine trade with England. Nowadays, Bordeaux has a cultural life expected of any major city as well as excellent shops.

Listed and protected by Unesco: the harmonious ensemble of Bordeaux' classicist old town

BORDEAUX

CITY WHERE TO START?
There are several underground car parks in the Old Town. Head for the **Esplanade des Quinconces** as most important sights are between here, the cathedral and the Garonne. The whole city centre is closed to traffic on the first Sun in the month. If you arrive by train, take tram C from the Gare Saint-Jean along the Garonne to the Quinconces stop opposite the Office de Tourisme.

SIGHTSEEING

CAPC MUSÉE D'ART CONTEMPORAIN DE BORDEAUX ⭐

Excellent collection of contemporary art. Some 700 trailblazing drawings, paintings, photos, installations and sculptures created since the 1970s are housed in the Centre d'Arts Plastiques Contemporains in an impressive warehouse that dates back to the early 19th century, the *Entrepôt Laîné. 7, Rue Ferrère | Tue–Sun 11am–6pm (Wed until 8pm) | www.capc-bordeaux.fr*

CATHÉDRALE SAINT-ANDRÉ

The Royal Gate depicting the 10 Apostles, the Ressurection and the Last Judgement, and the North Gate with the Last Supper, the Ascension and the Triumph of Christ are well worth seeing. *Place Jean Moulin*

LA CITÉ DU VIN ⭐ ●

Wine lovers can learn all about wine-growing and the ever-popular end results at the world of wine in the northern suburb of Bacalan (tram line B), which opened in 2016. Along with the modern form of imparting knowledge –

visitors are given a tablet as the digital companion through the 19 departments – the attractions include a restaurant and a wine bar, tastings and workshops: a veritable wine leisure park. The restaurant ☙ *Le 7 (closed Sun evening | tel. 05 64 31 05 40) on the seventh floor has wonderful views of the city. 134, Quai de Bacalan | July/Aug daily 9.30am–7.30pm, April–June and Sept/ Oct daily 9.30am–7pm, Nov–May Tue– Sun 10am–6pm | www.laciteduvin.com*

ESPLANADE DES QUINCONCES

This square, extending over more than 30 acres – one of the largest in Europe – was laid out in 1818–28 on the banks of the river. The column, almost 50 m/164 ft high, with its statue of liberty commemorates the Girondists who were executed. Two fountains decorated with bronze sculptures play at its base. The two other statues are of the writer Michel de Montaigne and the political thinker Baron de Montesquieu.

MUSÉE D'AQUITAINE

The history of Aquitaine can be traced in this museum which includes archeological finds and sections on wine growing and oyster farming. *20, Cours Pasteur | Tue–Sun 11am–6pm*

MUSÉE DES BEAUX ARTS

The completely refurbished Museum of Fine Arts contains a collection of paintings from the 17th to 20th centuries, including works by Rubens, Matisse, Picasso and Renoir. *20, Cours d'Albret | Wed–Mon 11am–18pm | www.musba-bordeaux.fr*

PLACE DE LA BOURSE

The elegant Place de la Bourse on the river promenade is flanked by the stock exchange on the north and the former custom's house (today's Custom's Museum) on the south side. A fountain with the Three Graces from the 19th century is a decorative central feature.

PLACE DE LA COMÉDIE

The magnificent *Grand Théâtre (tickets: tel. 05 56 00 85 95)*, built in 1773–80 in the Neo-Classicist style, dominates the square with the *Hôtel de Rolly*, also designed by the architect Victor Louis opposite.

TOUR PEY-BERLAND ⚜

A lovely view of the city can be enjoyed – after ascending 231 steps – from the viewing platform on the 47 m/154.2 ft-high bell tower adjoining cathedral. *Place Pey-Berland | June–Sept daily 10am–1.15pm and 2pm–6pm, Oct–May Tue–Sun 10am–12.30pm and 2pm–5.30pm | www.pey-berland.fr*

FOOD & DRINK

INSIDER TIP ▶ BELLE CAMPAGNE Ⓥ

Fresh seasonal ingredients from the south-west (the maximum distance to the kitchen is 250 km/155 mi, and all the producers are shown on the menu) feature on the menu in the trendy district of Saint-Pierre. Creative dishes are served upstairs, delicious finger food and wine downstairs. *Closed Sun/Mon and midday. | 15, Rue des Bahutiers | tel. 05 56 81 16 51 | www.belle-campagne.fr | Moderate*

CAFÉ DU THÉÂTRE

Delicious regional specialities such as braised shoulder of lamb with apricots can be found on the menu in this unpretentious bistro-style café-restaurant. *Closed Sun/Mon | 3, Square Jean Vauthier/Place Pierre Renaudel | tel. 05 57 95 77 20 | www.le-cafe-du-theatre.fr | Moderate*

The towers of Saint-André soar 81 m/266 ft up into the sky

LE CHAPON FIN

This gourmets' paradise, where the artist Henri de Toulouse-Lautrec and King Edward VII once dined, is an institution. The head chef, Nicolas Frion, a pupil of Paul Bocuse's, advocates a creative but classically French cuisine. *Closed Sun/Mon | 5, Rue Montesquieu | tel. 05 56 79 10 10 | www.chapon-fin.com | Expensive*

LE CHIEN DE PAVLOV
Even reading the menu, which changes with the seasons, in this bistro which is

Chartrons. *Closed Sun/Mon | 45, Rue Notre Dame | tel. 05 56 81 49 59 | www. chez-dupont.com | Moderate*

Haute culture in Bordeaux's opera house: the Neo-Classicist Grand Théâtre

run by two young Bordelaises will make your mouth water. Try the fried *foie gras* with cane sugar and celery! *Tue and Sun/ Mon closed. | 45–47, Rue de la Devise | tel. 05 56 48 26 71 | www.lechiendepavlov. com | Moderate*

COMPTOIR CUISINE
Stylish bistro opposite the Grand Théâtre, where the chic interior and modern, original interior harmonise perfectly. Three-course lunchtime menu Mon–Fri for under *20 euros! Daily | 2, Place de la Comédie | tel. 05 56 56 22 33 | www. comptoircuisine.com | Expensive*

CHEZ DUPONT
Regional classics from *foie gras* to mussel dishes in the trendy Quartier des

CHEZ JEAN
The unfussy interior of the brasserie allows diners to focus on the classics from the south-west and the wines from the region. Also serves excellent home-made burgers. *daily | Place du Parlement | tel. 05 56 44 44 43 | www.chezjeanbordeaux. fr | Budget–Moderate*

LE SAINT-JAMES
The excellent local cuisine of Nicolas Magie's team in Bouliac to the southeast of the city does not fall short in any way of its wonderful view over Bordeaux. A luxury hotel also belongs to this complex in the midst of vineyards. *Restaurant closed Sun/Mon | 3, Place Camille Hostein | Bouliac | tel. 05 56 44 27 68 | www.saint james-bouliac.com | Expensive*

LA TUPINA

Regional delicacies ranging from caviar from Aquitaine to duck from les Landes. A cauldron in which a hearty stew is usually simmering away, creates a rustic atmosphere in winter. It hangs over an open fire that forms a central feature in the restaurant. *Closed Mon | 6, Rue Porte de la Monnaie | tel. 05 56 91 56 37 | www.latupina.com | Moderate–Expensive*

SHOPPING

The pedestrian zone *Rue Sainte-Catherine* is the first address for fashion (e.g. *Galeries Lafayette*) and souvenirs. *Rue Notre-Dame* in the Chartron quarter is home to many antiques shops. Wearable (ladies') fashions made in Bordeaux are available from the designer boutique INSIDER TIP *Gianna et Moi (42, Rue Sainte-Colombe | www.giannaetmoi.com)*. Within the 'golden triangle' (*Allées de Tourny/Cours Clemenceau/Cours de l'Intendance*) there are a number of well-stocked wineshops. Wine tasting can be enjoyed in the *Maison du Vin de Bordeaux (1, Cours de 30 Juillet)* which also holds wine-making courses, and wine can be bought in the adjoining *vinotheque*. The food and delicatessen market *Marché des Quais* is held on Sun opposite the war cruiser 'Colbert' on Quai des Chartrons near Cours Martinique on the Garonne. The *market* is open Tue–Sun in the *Halles Les Capucins*.

ENTERTAINMENT

Live jazz and blues are played at the *I.Boat Le Restaurant (Quai Armand Lalande | Bassin à Flot)* and *Le Club House (59, Quai de Paludate)*. The *Opéra National de Bordeaux (tel. 05 56 00 85 95 | www.opera-bordeaux.com)* has a very good reputation and plays in three venues: opera is performed in the *Grand Théâtre*, operetta in *Théâtre Fémina (10, Rue de Grassi)* and symphony concerts at the *Auditorium de Bordeaux (9–13, Cours Georges Clemenceau)*. Techno and lounge music can be heard in *La Dame (1, Quai Armand Lalande | Bassin à Flot)*. The submarine base nearby, built by the Germans in World War II, where the stylish bar and brasserie *Le Café Maritime (Quai Lalande | Bassin à Flot)* can also be found, has developed into a INSIDER TIP popular place for a night out.

WHERE TO STAY

BLUE LODGE

Charming, well-maintained guesthouse close to the city centre with a garden and four individually furnished rooms. So it's essential to book well in advance for summer! *70, Rue de Ségur | tel. 06 78 25 85 83 | www.bluelodgeinbordeaux.com | Moderate*

INSIDER TIP AU CŒUR DE BORDEAUX

This beautifully restored 19th century building close to the cathedral contains five room furnished with antiques and unusual accessories. The hosts offer wine tastings with tapas in their wine cellar. *28, Rue Boulan | tel. 06 89 65 84 21 | www.aucoeurdebordeaux.fr | Moderate*

GRAND HÔTEL

The no. 1 address in the best location opposite the opera house offers complete luxury in all 150 of its rooms, from carefully selected furniture and fabrics to marble bathrooms. *2–5, Place de la Comédie | tel. 05 57 30 44 44 | www.ghbordeaux.com | Expensive*

LA MAISON DU LIERRE

Elegant hotel within ancient walls with an enchanting garden close to the "golden triangle". *12 rooms | 57, Rue Huguerie | tel. 05 56 51 92 71 | www.maisondulierre. com | Expensive*

LA TOUR INTENDANCE

This hotel with its stylish contemporary furnishings, lovely wooden floors and partially exposed stone walls, is right in the thick of things. *36 rooms | 14–16, Rue de la Vieille Tour | tel. 05 56 44 56 56 | www.hotel-tour-intendance.com | Budget– Expensive*

WHERE TO GO

BLAYE (140 C2) (*ØJ E10*)

A vast citadel completed in 1689 is the main attraction in this little town (pop. 5000) 45 km/28 mi north of Bordeaux on the Gironde. Inside the citadel a craft village and eateries have been established. Otherwise everything in Blaye revolves around wine, especially red wine. The *Maison du Vin de Blaye (12, Cours Vauban | Mon 10am–12.30pm*

As charming as the rest of the little (wine) town: Place Principale in Saint-Émilion

LA VILLA BORDELAISE

Small hotel only 10 minutes from the old town in a beautifully restored building, around 100 years old, with a small garden and a terrace – ideal for travellers seeking peace and quiet. *2 rooms | 48, Rue des Frères Faucher | tel. 05 56 58 27 63 | www.lescinqsens-bordeaux.com | Expensive*

INFORMATION

12, Cours du XXX Juillet | tel. 05 56 00 6600 | www.bordeaux-tourisme.com

and 2pm–6.30pm, Tue–Sat 8.30am– 12.30pm and 2pm–6.30pm | www.vin- blaye.com) presents an overview.

CHÂTEAU DE LA BRÈDE (140 C4) (*ØJ E12*)

The state theorist Charles Louis de Secondat, Baron de la Brède et de Montesquieu (1689–1755), grew up in this castle in the little town of the same name (pop. 3500), 18 km/11.2 mi south of Bordeaux. The moated castle is still owned by the family today, and some of the rooms are open to the public. *Mid*

April–May and Oct–mid Nov Sat/Sun 2pm–6pm, June and Sept Wed–Mon 2pm–6pm, July/Aug 10am–6pm | www.chateaulabrede.com

CHÂTEAU MONTAIGNE

(141 D3) (*Ø G11*)

Michel de Montaigne (1533–1592) retired from the pressures of life on his 38th birthday to the library tower on his estate to find more peace to write. For nine years he did not leave the tower. The result: three volumes of his famous Essais. These have led to the tower, some 50 km/30 mi to the east of Bordeaux, becoming a much-visited site today. The castle burnt down in the 19th century and was rebuilt; the tower was preserved. Tower July/Aug daily 11am–5.15pm, April–June and Sept Wed–Sun 11am, 3pm, 4pm and 5.15pm, park July/Aug daily 10am–6.30pm, April–June and Sept/Oct Wed–Sun 10–noon and 2pm–6.30pm, otherwise 5.30pm, closed Jan | www.chateau-montaigne.com

CHÂTEAU SMITH-HAUT LAFITTE

(140 C3) (*Ø E12*)

Wine doesn't just taste good, it also makes you beautiful – well, that's the motto of the wine spa hotel ● Les Sources de Caudalie (61 rooms and suites | tel. 05 57 83 83 83 | www.sources-caudalie.com | Expensive). Dine like royalty amongst the vineyards of this château 20 km/12.4 mi south of Bordeaux, and look after your health and beauty as well with treatments such as Peeling à la Sauvignon or a wine massage.

SAINT-ÉMILION ★ (141 D3) (*Ø F11*)

This little old town (pop. 2000) is situated on two hills 40 km/24.9 mi east of Bordeaux. The charming traffic-free (although very busy) old town and well-stocked wine shops are as much a part of its attractions as the underground church that has been carved out of the rock Église Monolithe, the catacombs and the Chapelle de la Trinité from the 9th-13th centuries.

Regional cuisine and a tremendous selection of wines are yours to enjoy at the brasserie Amelia Canta (daily | 2, Place de l'Église Monolithe | tel. 05 57 74 48 03 | www.ameliacanta.com | Budget). The restaurant of the elegant Hostellerie de Plaisance (17 rooms and 4 suites | restaurant closed Sun/Mon | Place du Clocher | tel. 05 57 55 07 55 | www.hostellerie-plaisance.com | Expensive) contained within the walls of a former monastery is run by Ronan Kervarrec, award-winning chef from Brittany. INSIDER TIP Château Franc Mayne (9 rooms | 14, La Gomerie | tel. 05 57 24 62 61 | www.chateaufrancmayne.com | Expensive) is beautifully furnished and guests can enjoy the privilege of sampling the château's own wines. Information: Place des Créneaux | tel. 05 57 55 28 28 | www.saint-emilion-tourisme.com

MIMIZAN

(142 C2) (*Ø D13–14*) **The pretty holiday resort of Mimizan (pop. 700) south of the Étang d'Aureilhan made this section of the coast famous in the 1920s.**

Early summer visitors included Coco Chanel, Winston Churchill, Charlie Chaplin and Salvador Dalí. Although it is 6 km/3.7 mi from Mimizan-Plage to Mimizan-Bourg, the two are becoming ever closer. Plage is an idyllic holiday location with a pedestrian precinct, a promenade along the riverbank, a comprehensive range of watersports facilities and five wide beaches. The 7 km/4.4 mi watercourse, the Courant de Mimizan, links the lake with the sea and divides Mimizan's 10 km/6.2 mi beach into a northern and southern section. There are more than 300 types of plants on the 'Flower Promenade' *Rue du Lac*. Mimizan-Bourg inland is where the municipal offices are concentrated as well as industry in the form of a paper factory that, unfortunately, can be smelt from miles around.

SIGHTSEEING

MUSÉE D'HISTOIRE DE MIMIZAN
The local museum documents the history of the area, how the forest was used and professions such as that of the sawmill worker, the gum-tapper and the donkey driver. *Rue de l'Abbaye | mid June–mid Sept Mon–Sat, otherwise Mon–Fri after making an appointment in advance, tel. 05 58 09 00 61 at 10am, 11am, 2pm, 3pm and 4pm | www.musee. mimazan.com*

PRIEURÉ BÉNÉDICTINE
In the mid 17th century, the Benedictine monks abandoned the abbey situated on the road between Mimizan and Mimizan-Plage that had been so important in the Middle Ages. 100 years later it was buried under a 'migrating' dune –

only the bell tower stuck out of the sand. With its carved portal from the 13th century, it is now a Unesco World Heritage Site. *musee.mimizan.com*

FOOD & DRINK

LE BISTROT DE LA MER
Seafood and fish in a pleasant interior. *closed Mon | 8, Av. Maurice Martin | tel. 05 58 09 08 56 | Budget–Moderate*

L'ÎLE DE MALTE
Typical regional specialities with old pictures of Mimizan on the walls. *Closed Tue evening, Sun evening and Wed | 5, Rue du Casino | tel. 05 58 82 48 15 | Budget*

A NOSTE ☙
Fish and seafood with a view of the beach. *Daily | 7, Boluevard de la Côte d'Argent | tel. 05 58 09 31 34 | www. anoste.fr | Budget*

LA TABLE DE LA FERME
Good regional cuisine and a pretty garden in the pedestrian zone. *Daily | 31, Av. Maurice Martin | tel. 05 58 09 27 81 | www.tabledelaferme-restaurant-mim izan.fr | Moderate*

LOW BUDGET

Admission to the *Musée d'Aquitaine and the Musée des Beaux Arts* in Bordeaux is free on the first Sunday of the month except in July and August.

Why not visit one of the famous wine-producers in Médoc? Almost all tours are free and you really learn a lot about viniculture.

SHOPPING

Daily *food market* in the market hall, and an *evening market* with crafts, clothing and regional products on Tuesdays and Saturdays in July and August on the Place du Marché.

SPORTS & ACTIVITIES

Apart from virtually all types of sport on or in water, horse riding and golf also belong to the extensive range of things to do here.

CÔTE D'ARGENT

ENTERTAINMENT

No seaside resort does without its gambling den. In addition to the *casino* in *Rue du Casino*, popular clubs include *Bar Américain (19, Rue Brémontier)* and *Le Gwadinina (2, Av. de la Jetée)*.

WHERE TO STAY

CAMPING CLUB MARINA-LANDES
In a pine forest with direct access to the beach; shops, swimming pool, restaurant, pizzeria, bike rental and a children's playground. *573 pitches | Rue Marina | Plage Sud | tel. 05 58 09 12 66 | www.marinalandes.com*

L'ÉMERAUDE DES BOIS
The hotel (and its restaurant) are on the banks of the Courant, just a 5-minutes drive from the beach and the town. *17 rooms | 66/68, Av. de Courant | Plage Sud | tel. 05 58 09 05 28 | www.emeraude desbois.com | Budget*

HÔTEL DE FRANCE
Basic, but close to the beach – some rooms with sea views! – and pleasant staff. *21 rooms | 18, Av. de la Côte d'Argent | tel. 05 58 09 09 01 | www. hoteldefrance-mimizan.com | Budget*

INSIDER TIP ECOLODGE SEGOSA
A former barn has been converted and furnished to exacting enviromental standard to create this small hotel in the little village of Saint-Paul-en-Born, 10 minutes from the coast. With natural thermal regulation, the use of locally sourced natural materials and renewable energy sources, the owners have gone way beyond doing away with clean towels every day to ensure a sustainable economic management. But guests do not have to do without any

creature comforts or style. *14 rooms | Route de Mezos | Saint-Paul-en-Born | tel. 06 89 49 58 84 | Budget*

Please respect the bathing zones: the ocean is tremendously powerful

INFORMATION

38, Av. Maurice Martin | tel. 05 58 09 11 20 | www.mimizan-tourisme.com

WHERE TO GO

CONTIS-PLAGE (142 C2) (∅ C–D14)
This tiny resort is 23 km/14.3 mi south of Mimizan, on the Courant de Contis estuary. The lovely long beaches are perfect for a quiet and relaxing beach holiday. The pride of the resort is the

☼ lighthouse (July/Aug Tue–Sun 10am–noon and 3pm–7pm, April–June and Sept Sat/Sun 2pm–6pm), which was built in 1862 – and no wonder, because it is the only one on the entire stretch of coast between Cap Ferret and Capbreton. 183 steps take you up to wonderful panoramic views along the coast and the forest beyond. *Information: 201, Route des Lacs | Saint-Julien-en-Born | tel. 05 58 42 89 80 | www.cotelandesnaturetourisme.com*

COURANT D'HUCHET ★
(142 C3) (𝄞 C15)

This nature reserve around the Courant d'Huchet is 40 km/24.9 mi south of Mimizan. The little river flows through a forested landscape and enters the sea near Huchet. Hikes are available from *Pichelèbe. To book: tel. 05 58 48 73 91 | www.reservenaturelle-couranthuchet.org*

ÉCOMUSÉE DE MARQUÈZE
(143 D2) (𝄞 E14)

It is worth travelling the 45 km/28 mi inland just to visit this open-air museum. A tiny historic railway takes you from Sabres directly to the marsh and heathland of the 19th century. At the museum village of *Marquèze*, farmers with ox carts till the fields, a water mill tinkling in the background, while the aroma of freshly-baked bread from the baker's fills the air: a museum for all the senses. *April–Sept daily, greatly staggered times, peak time 2pm–4.40pm every 40 min, last return 6pm, July/Aug 10.10am–5.20pm continuously | www.marqueze.fr*

LÉON (142 C3) (𝄞 D15)
This pretty holiday resort (pop. 1500) 40 km/24.9 mi south of Mimizan is on the Lac de Léon and 7 km/4.4 mi from the sea. The comprehensive range of activities on offer (golf, surfing and sailing schools, riding and swimming in the lake) is perfect for families with children. The campsite *Lou Puntaou (1315, Av. du Lac | tel. 05 58 48 74 30 | www.loupuntaou.com)* with 391 pitches is here by the lake, 20 acres with a large outdoor pool, children's club, bar and restaurant. *Information: 65, Place Jean Baptiste Courtiau | tel. 05 58 48 76 03 | www.leon.fr*

MOLIETS-ET-MAÂ (142 C3) (𝄞 C15)
Another relatively quiet, family-friendly resort south of Mimizan (47 km/29.2 mi) is Moliets-et-Maâ. Its attractions include a lake, lots of pine trees and the beach at Moliets-Plage just 2.5 km/1.6 mi away. Moliets-et-Maâ has an attractive centre with pretty old buildings, a church and a chapel. The sports and leisure activity programme is extensive. There are hiking trails through the forest, fishing grounds, a golf course, an aerial ropeway, riding clubs, tennis courts, a skatepark and of course every conceivable type of watersport. *Information: Rue du Général Cau-nègre | tel. 05 58 48 56 58 | www.moliets.com*

VIEUX-BOUCAU-LES-BAINS
(142 B–C3) (𝄞 C15)

This village 54 km/33.6 mi south of Mimizan was a not unimportant port, known as Port d'Albret, until the largest river in les Landes, the Adour, was diverted to Bayonne in the 16th century. Vieux-Boucau (pop. 1400) is now a lively holiday destination with attractive half-timbered buildings in its traffic-free centre, a lake, dunes, new holiday houses and the promenade *Le Mail. La Côte d'Argent (30 rooms | 4, Grand'Rue | tel. 05 58 48 13 17 | www.lacotedargent-vieuxboucau.fr | Budget)* is a pleasant hotel in the pedestrian precinct. *Information: 11, Mail André Rigal | tel. 05 58 48 13 47 | www.ot-vieux-boucau.fr*

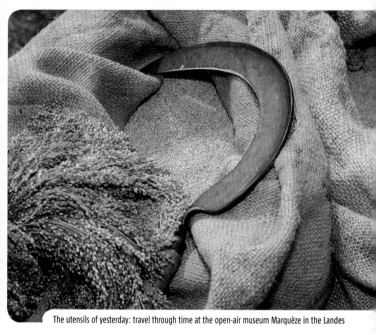

The utensils of yesterday: travel through time at the open-air museum Marquèze in the Landes

PAUILLAC

(140 B1) (*∅ E10*) **The Médoc peninsula on the western bank of the Gironde is anchored in the minds of every lover of red wine the whole world over.**

Visitors to the largest village, ★ *Pauillac* (pop. 5000), with its 23 *châteaux*, mid way between the coast and Bordeaux, should have a car with as big a boot as possible! There is also a lovely beach, an elegant marina and many opportunities for watersports.

SIGHTSEEING

CHÂTEAUX ●

Almost all the *châteaux* are open to the public except in the grape-picking season. Visits must always be booked in ad-vanced, either directly at the winery or through the Office du Tourisme. The most famous places include *Château Lafite-Roth-schild (no tel. | www.lafite.com)*, *Château Latour (tel. 05 56 73 19 80 | www.cha-teau-latour.com)*, *Château Pichon-Longue-ville (tel. 05 56 73 17 17 | www. pichon longueville.com)*, *Château Lynch-Bages (tel. 05 56 73 24 00 | www.jmcazes.com)*, *Château Les Carmes Haut-Brion (tel. 05 56 93 23 40 | www.les-carmes-haut-brion. com)* and *Château Gaudin (tel. 05 56 59 24 93 | www.chateau-gaudin.fr)*; in this family-run business you can INSIDER TIP cork and label a bottle yourself. There's a "diploma" and the bottle as souvenirs.

In one sense, the Rolls-Royce of the wine castles, and with its own museum on the history of wine is: *Château Mou-ton-Rothschild (tel. 05 56 73 21 29 | www.chateau-mouton-rothschild.com)*.

FOOD & DRINK

CORDEILLAN BAGES
Gourmet cuisine in the eponymous hotel of the Relais & Châteaux Group. Chef de cuisine Jean-Luc Rocha holds two Michelin stars. *Closed Sat noon and Mon/Tue | Route des Châteaux | tel. 05 56 59 24 24 | www.cordeillanbages. com | Expensive*

INSIDER TIP CAFÉ LAVINAL
The owner of Château Lynch-Bages, Jean-Michel Cazes, bought and restored his native village of *Bages* south of Pauillac which had been virtually completely deserted. It now has a baker, shops and this bistro which serves regional fare. *Closed Sun evenings | Place Desquet | tel. 05 57 75 00 09 | Moderate*

SHOPPING

As well as wine, there's a pretty market *(Sat morning | Place du Marché)*. The vinotheque of the Maison du Tourisme et du Vin displays and sells 300 of the total of 1500 wines of the Médoc – at the same price as in the *châteaux*.

WHERE TO STAY

CHÂTEAU POMYS
If you don't want to drive after the wine tasting, you can stay here on the estate. *10 rooms | Route de Poumeys Saint-Estèphe | tel. 05 56 59 73 44 | www. chateaupomys.com | Moderate*

HÔTEL DE FRANCE ET D'ANGLETERRE
This hotel with a pretty garden and a restaurant is on the Gironde estuary. *48 rooms | 3, Quai Albert Pichon | tel. 05 56 59 01 20 | www.hoteldefrance-angle terre.com | Budget*

INFORMATION

La Verrerie | tel. 05 56 59 03 08 | www. pauillac-medoc.com

WHERE TO GO

HOURTIN (140 A1) (*∅ D10*)
This village (pop. 3250) 25 km/15.5 mi west of Pauillac is divided into the three parts Plage, Lac and the marina Port. The *Lac d'Hourtin et de Carcans*, the largest natural inland lake in France, is a mecca for watersports enthusiasts. Hourtin has been awarded the 'Station Kid' title thanks to its 24-acre, traffic-free 'children's island'.

A peaceful and friendly establishment is the *Hotel Les Pins (18 rooms | 22, Rue de Mauricet | tel. 05 56 09 18 07 | www. hotellespins-hourtin.com | Budget)* on the outskirts of the village, and with an outdoor pool. A campsite 300 m/984 ft from the ocean and 4 km/2.5 mi from the lake in a pine forest, with a pool, gym, mini club, numerous sporting activities and a restaurant is *La Côte d'Argent (Rue d'Aquitaine | tel. 05 56 09 10 25 | www.camping-cote-dargent.com)*. *www.medococean.com*

LACANAU-OCÉAN
(140 A2) (*∅ D11*)
The more than 14 km/8 mi beach with its high dunes, the Lac de Lacanau and dense pine forests are the plus points of this village (pop. 3400) a good 50 km/31.1 mi to the southwest. Lacanau is one of the major seaside resorts on the Côte d'Argent offering every conceivable type of watersport, 3 golf courses, 3 riding schools and an extensive network of cycle paths and hiking trails. Information: *Place de l'Europe | tel. 05 56 03 21 01 | www. medococean.com*

MONTALIVET-LES-BAINS
(138 B6) *(∅ D10)*

This village (pop. 1900), almost 40 km/ 25 mi to the northwest of Pauillac, has been popular among nudists since the 1950s. Apart from in dedicated holiday complexes, nude bathing is tolerated on 2600) on the Côte d'Argent, a good 50 km/30 mi north of Pauillac, combines all the plus points of the 'Silver Coast' – dunes, the pine forest, the sea and a casino. The *Plage Centrale* is protected by a sandbank and groynes. *Océan Hôtel Amélie (21 rooms | tel.*

These grapes have a tremendous career ahead of them: rows of vines at Château Lafite-Rothschild

the *Plage du Gressier. Euronat (Grayan-L'Hôpital | tel. 05 56 09 33 33 | www.euro nat.fr)*, Europe's largest nudist colony, is 5 km/3 mi away and has its own thalassotherapy centre. Information: *62, Av. de l'Océan | Vendays Montalivet | tel. 05 56 09 30 12 | www.ot-vendays-montalivet.fr*

SOULAC-SUR-MER (138 B5) *(∅ D9)*

The most northerly seaside resort (pop. *05 56 09 78 05 | www.oceanhotelame lie.com | Moderate)*, with a pretty garden, pool and play area, is in a forest 900 m/2952 ft from the beach, and is run by a couple who are originally from Switzerland. There is a car ferry 9 km/ 5.6 mi to the north-east at Le Verdon-sur-Mer across the Gironde estuary. Information: *68, Rue de la Plage | tel. 05 56 09 86 61 | www.soulac.com*

CÔTE BASQUE

The landscape changes shortly before Biarritz: the country's wide beaches, fringed by expensive pine forests, are replaced by the rockier Basque coast, which is only 30 km/18.6 mi long (on the French side).

And it becomes more glamourous too. The wealthy have been coming to Biarritz since time immemorial. Originally it was European aristocrats, nowadays it is film stars and the *nouveau riche*. And Saint-Jean-de-Luz has less to do with seaside resorts so familiar further up the Atlantic coast and more with elegant holiday destinations on the Mediterranean.

Many signs are in two languages – French and *Euskara* (Basque) – with a noticeable number of 'x's 'k's suddenly appearing. But unlike on the Spanish side, there is no separatist movement in the French part of the Basque Country. The only wish that is expressed from time to time is to have a département of their own. The Basque language that was once in danger of becoming extinct, is now being carefully nurtured.

BIARRITZ

MAP INSIDE BACK COVER
(142 B5) (*C16*) **Hydrangeas in bloom, steep alleyways, lovely shops and views everywhere of the sea: the resort and surfer eldorado Biarritz (pop. 25,000) is a jewel on the French Atlantic Coast.**

Elegant seaside towns on a rugged coastline: exclusive resorts, picturesque fishing villages and the Pyrenees waiting to be explored

Biarritz, where the sun shines on the Grande Plage 2000 hours a year, has given its glory-of-old a fresh glamourous look. Napoleon III and his empress Eugénie – who fell in love with the fishing port long before she got married – made it fashionable. The royal household accompanied them en vacances and soon kings and tzars dropped by, and Biarritz became a meeting place for high society.

As well as thalassotherapy, golf and surfing, the city's tourist attractions include Basque pelota – and you simply must see this game being played, as it's such a huge part of the Basque identity – and also the Basque rural sports.

The "grande dame" of the bathing resorts is manageable, but it gets pretty busy during the season, and parking (there is a charge) in the centre is a constant challenge. The old town is small, and you can easily walk to the museums, the market hall, the beaches and the old harbour...

SIGHTSEEING

INSIDER TIP ▶ ASIATICA MUSÉE D'ART ASIATIQUE

With more than 1000 exhibits from India, Tibet, Nepal and China, this is one of das and colourful coral fish ensure that any visit is an unforgettable experience. *Esplanade du Rocher de la Vierge | for opening-hours see homepage, April–Oct daily 9.30am–8pm, July/Aug until midnight | www.aquariumbiarritz.com*

We don't think any other museum has a shop that is as popular as the one at Planète du Chocolat

the most important museums of Asian art in Europe. *1, Rue Guy Petit | July/Aug and french holidays Mon–Fri 10.30am–6.30pm, Sat/Sun 2pm–7pm, Mon–Fri 2pm–6.30pm, Sat/Sun 2pm–7pm | www.museeasiatica.com*

BIARRITZ AQUARIUM ★

The modernised, 1.7 acres museum is a fascinating experience, not just for families. The main focuses include the sea worlds of Biscay and the Caribbean, which are represented by more than 300 species in twelve aquariums and an 11 m/36 ft lagoon. The visit continues to Cape Horn and the Pacific, where you can see sharks and rays. Huge moray eels, reef and hammerhead sharks, barracu-

CHAPELLE IMPÉRIALE

The imperial chapel was built for Empress Eugénie in 1864 in the Romanesque and Byzantine style with Moorish elements. *Rue Pellot | June–Sept Thu and Sat, April/May and Oct Sat 2.30pm–6pm, March and Nov/Dec Sat 2.30pm–5pm*

CITÉ DE L'OCÉAN

This hands-on museum, designed by the New York architect Steven Holl in the shape of a wave, focuses on all aspects of marine research and protection. How the oceans were created and why man is dependent on them, for example, are explained in an informative and entertaining way. The section devoted to the secrets and sagas of the sea is particularly thrilling – such as the notorious Bermuda Triangle and the Flood in the Bible. *1, Av. de la Plage | greatly staggered times, see website, April–Oct daily 10am–7pm, July/Aug until 10pm | www.citedelocean.com*

MUSÉE HISTORIQUE DE BIARRITZ
The history of the town's beginnings and its heyday presented in the former Anglican church. *Rue Broquedis | Tue–Sat 10am–12.30pm and 2pm–6.30pm | www.musee-historique-biarritz.fr*

PHARE SAINT-MARTIN ✕
Built in 1834, the 73 m/239.5 ft-high white lighthouse is situated on Mont Saint-Martin that divides the sandy beaches of les Landes from the rocky Basque coastline. After climbing the 248 steps, you will be rewarded with a superb view all the way to Spain. *May/June and Sept daily 2pm–6pm, July/Aug 10am–1.30pm and 2pm–7pm, Oct–April Sat/Sun, French school holidays daily 2pm–5pm*

PLANÈTE MUSÉE DU CHOCOLAT
The history and art of chocolate-making. *14, Av. Beaurivage | July/Aug daily 10am–7pm, Sept–June, Mon–Sat 10am–12.30pm and 2.30pm–6.30pm | www.planetemuseeduchocolat.com*

ROCHER DE LA VIERGE ✕
An iron bridge connects the rock in the turbulent waters to the mainland. The statue of the Virgin Mary has perched atop the rock since 1865.

FOOD & DRINK

CHEZ ALBERT ✕
Fish and seafood on the old fishing harbour. *Closed Wed | 51 bis, Allée Port des Pêcheurs | tel. 05 59 24 43 84 | www.chezalbert.fr | Expensive*

INSIDER TIP L'ATELIER DE GAZTELUR
A few kilometres outside on an historic estate in the countryside, Alexandre Bousquet runs an antiques shop and a flower studio that also offers courses in hand-tying flowers, in addition to his award-winning cuisine that uses products from the south-west. *Closed Sun/Mon | Arcangues | Chemin de Gastelhur | tel. 05 59 23 04 06 | gaztelur.com | Expensive*

BALEAK
Traditional Basque cuisine with imaginative fish specialities is served in a friendly, brightly-lit restaurant near the market.

MARCO POLO HIGHLIGHTS

⭐ **Grande Plage in Biarritz**
The main beach in Biarritz is one of the most elegant and beautiful in Europe → p. 88

⭐ **Hôtel du Palais in Biarritz**
Treat yourself to an apéritif in this legendary hotel – the glamourous flair comes free of charge → p. 89

⭐ **Hossegor**
This surfing eldorado is one of the most beautiful beaches on the Atlantic Coast → p. 91

⭐ **Saint-Jean-de-Luz**
Let yourself be taken in by the magical atmosphere of this romantic little town → p. 92

⭐ **Biarritz Aquarium**
The modern interactive aquarium will turn you into an amateur marine biologist → p. 86

⭐ **Corniche Basque**
Fabulous coastal route → p. 95

Except for July/Aug closed Sun evening and Mon, July/Aug daily, but closed at lunchtime | 8, Rue du Centre | tel. 05 59 24 58 57 | www.baleak.fr | Moderate

INSIDER TIP CARO SUSHI

Affordable sushi made from freshly-caught fish and other culinary delights from the fish stalls in the market hall. *April–Dec Tue–Sun 8am–1.30pm | tel. 06 82 08 71 86 | Budget*

INSIDER TIP COMPTOIR DU FOIE GRAS

Wine is enjoyed at standing tables outside the door, and the kitchen of this tiny bar (also a shop that sells regional specialities) next to the market hall serves fabulous tapas and, of course, *foie gras*. Good selection of wines, sweet and hearty breakfasts in the morning. *closed Mon | 1, Rue du Centre | tel. 05 59 22 57 42 | www.comptoir-du-foie-gras. com | Budget*

BAR JEAN

Right next to the market halls; breakfast and tapas; ideal for watching the world go by. *Daily | 5, Rue des Halles | tel. 05 59 24 80 38 | www.barjean-biarritz.fr | Budget*

LA PLANCHA ILBARRITZ

Situated a little to the south in Bidart. This is the place to meet for a sundowner. *Closed Wed | Av. du Lac/Plage d'Ilbaritz | tel. 05 59 23 44 95 | Budget*

SHOPPING

The offer in Biarritz is irresistible. Every morning, the ● market (fish, food) attracts visitors to the two halls, where music plays; in summer there are stands outside selling clothing. In July and August there is an evening market in the market hall and surrounding streets on Wednesdays. Colourful Basque tableware, not just in the traditional striped patterns, is available e.g. from *Euskal Linge (14, Rue Mazagran)*, delicious cheese from *Mille et un Fromages (8, Av. Victor Hugo)*. Chocolates and lots of other tasty treats are made by *Chocolatier Henriet (Place Clemenceau)*. The irresistible products from *Miremont (Place Bellevue | www.miremont-biarritz.com)*, which also has a **INSIDER TIP** very stylish salon de thé, are worth countless sins. Do try their hot chocolate! Culinary souvenirs of all kinds are available from the *épicerie Maison Arostéguy (5, Av. Victor Hugo | www.arosteguy.com)*.

SPORTS & BEACHES

The largest and most beautiful beach is the ★ *Grande Plage*, that runs from the Hotel du Palais to Bellevue. The sea here however is anything but tame – which makes is excellent for surfing. Surfing is forbidden on *Plage Miramar* due to the strong currents. Surfers love the *Plage de la Côte des Basques*. The *Plage du Port Vieux* is a relatively small but sheltered beach and is suitable for swimming. But that's what a lot of dogs think too. *La Marbella* and *La Milady* beaches – that are also surfers' territory – are more glamourous.

Surfing is as much a part of Biarritz as salt is to the sea. Several schools offer courses. There are 10 golf courses in and around Biarritz. Riders head for *Club Hippique de Biarritz (Allée Gabrielle Dorziat | tel. 05 59 23 52 33 | www.biar ritzcheval.com)*. 3 diving schools are located in the Port des Pêcheurs; a heated seawater pool for cooler weather can be found in the casino building. Anyone wanting to try their hand at pelota should contact *Fronton Euskal-Jaï (Allée d'Aguilera | tel. 05 59 23 91 09 | www. cesta-punta.com)*.

Spain is really not far away: tapas in Bar Jean near the market in Biarritz

ENTERTAINMENT

The *Bar Royalty (Place Clemenceau)* has a lovely terrace, and appeals to a young audience. There a lots of bars in Port Vieux, which is also popular with a young audience. The Art déco *casino* on the promenade is also home to the *Café des Sports*. Also on the promenade is the club ✂ *Carré Coast (www.lecarrecoast.com)*, which has sea views. Other popular clubs are the *Duplex (24, Av. Edouard VII)*, the *Le Caveau (4, Rue Gambetta)*, which has a gay and hetero audience, the popular *Playboy Club (Rue Monhaut)* and the *Blue Cargo (Av. Ilbaritz) i*n Bidart. Another trendy meeting place with a gay audience is the chic *Bô Bar (26, Rue Gambetta)*.

WHERE TO STAY

ALCYON

Small hotel with a pretty and cheerful breakfast room. *15 rooms | 8, Rue Maison Suisse | tel. 05 59 22 64 60 | www.hotel-alcyon-biarritz.com | Moderate–Expensive*

HÔTEL ANJOU

Simply furnished but friendly and well-looked-after hotel 300 m/984 ft from the beach. Some rooms have balconies and/or a view of the sea. *30 rooms | 18, Rue Gambetta | tel. 05 59 24 00 93 | www.hotel-anjou-biarritz.com | Moderate–Expensive*

LES BAIGNEUSES DE BIARRITZ ✂

This small hotel is on the beach at the old harbour. Basque dishes are served in the restaurant or on the large terrace in nice weather. *10 rooms., 2 suites | 14, Rue du Port Vieux | tel. 05 59 24 41 84 | www.lesbaigneusesdebiarritz.com | Expensive*

HÔTEL DU PALAIS ★

Sleep like royalty: this establishment, which is one of the „Leading Hotels of the World", was the summer residence of Napoleon III and Empress Eugénie, and is a magnificent as you would expect. It has a pool, a spa, an award-winning restaurant *Villa Eugénie*, one other restaurant and two bars. *132 rooms. |*

The towers of Sainte-Marie's cathedral dominate the Old Town of Bayonne

1, Av. de l'Impératrice | tel. 05 59 41 64 00 | www.hotel-du-palais.com | Expensive

HÔTEL SAINT JULIEN

Lovely 19th-century hotel stylishly furnished in pastel shades. Its small garden is an oasis of peace and quiet in the heart of Biarritz. Guests have free use of the private car park. Some of the ✿ rooms on the 3rd floor have a view of the sea. *20 rooms | 20, Av. Carnot | tel. 05 59 24 20 39 | www.saint-julien-biarritz.com | Expensive*

INSIDER TIP HÔTEL DE SILHOUETTE

In the 17th century, this was home to Étienne de Silhouette, one of the ministers of Louis XV; today the villa is a hotel. Almost impossible to see from the road, it is situated in a lovely garden with a large terrace. The interior is tastefully understated. Some of the roooms have ✿ balconies with sea views. *20 rooms | 30, Rue Gambetta | tel. 05 59 24 93 82 | www.hotelsilhouette.com | Expensive*

INFORMATION

Square d'Ixelles | tel. 05 59 22 37 10 | www.biarritz.fr

WHERE TO GO

BAYONNE (142 B5) (𝑚 C16)

The port of Bayonne (pop. 47,000) on the lower Adour was a free trading area from 1784 onwards and an important hub in dealings with the Antilles, Spain and Holland. The arms business also helped the town 10 km/6.2 mi east of Biarritz to riches – it was here that the bayonet was invented and sold in huge numbers around the globe.

The beautiful Old Town is well worth seeing as are the Gothic Cathedrale *Sainte-Marie (Place Pasteur | daily 8am–12.30pm and 3pm–7pm, Sun until 8pm)* and the ● Musée Basque et de l'Histoire de Bayonne *(37, Quai des Corsaires | July/Aug Fri–Wed 10am–6.30pm, Thu 10am–8.30pm, April–June and Sept Tue–Sun 10am–6.30pm, Oct–March 10.30am–6pm | www.musee-basque.com)* that is devoted to the Basque culture. It's also well worth visiting the *Musée Bonnat (5, Rue Jacques Laffitte | www.musee-bonnat.com)*, which has works by Goya, Rubens, Degas and El Greco, although it is currently closed for extensive refurbishments.

Bayonne's Old Town, with its proud patricians' houses and Basque half-timbering with colourful shutters, is an attractive and lively place to stroll around and go shopping. A lot of ● *chocolatiers* can be found here too, e.g. *Atelier du Chocolat (7, Allée de Gibéléou | www.atelierduchoc*

olat.fr) and several other tempting addresses on *Rue Port-Neuf*, ever since cocoa was unloaded in the port here in the 17th century.

The former professional pelota player Jean-Pierre Marmouyet has decorated his restaurant *Le Chistera (closed Mon | 42, Rue Port-Neuf | tel. 05 59 59 25 93 | www. lechistera.com | Budget)* with all sorts of sports paraphernalia, and serves down-to-earth Basque fare at very reasonable prices. The nicest place to sit is outside under the 200-year-old arcades. The food served in the Michelin Star restaurant *Auberge du Cheval Blanc (closed Sat lunchtime, Sun evening and Mon | 68, Rue Bourgneuf | tel. 05 59 59 01 33 | www.cheval-blanc-bay onne.com | Moderate–Expensive)* is ambitious and with a regional touch. Information: *Place des Basques | tel. 05 59 46 09 00 | www.bayonne-tourisme.com*

CAPBRETON (142 B4) (*♒ C15*)

The bathing resort, fishing harbour and marina (pop. 8000), with a wide range of facilities for watersports enthusiasts, 19 tennis courts and a casino, is 25 km/15.5 mi north of Biarritz. *Hôtel Porto Rico (20 rooms | 4, Rue de Madrid | tel. 05 58 41 38 63 | www.hotelportorico.*

com | Budget)* is a welcoming place to stay, furnished in a sleek contemporary style, just 50 m/164 ft from the beach and port with a garden and private car park. Information: *Av. du Président Pompidou | tel. 05 58 72 12 11 | www.capbret on-tourisme.com*

DAX (142 C4) (*♒ D15*)

Even the Romans came here to take the waters. France's oldest spa (pop. 20,000) is a good 50 km/30 mi northeast of Biarritz. Dax is still famous for its thermal springs and several Roman remains can be seen too. Information: *11, Cours Foch | tel. 05 58 56 86 86 | www. dax-tourisme.com*

HOSSEGOR ★ (142 B4) (*♒ C15*)

Hossegor (pop. 4000) is only separated from Capbreton to the south by a tributary of the Adour. Before it reaches its mouth the river widens to form Lac d'Hossegor where celebrities and the well-off settled in the 1920s and '30s around the shore. Today it is the heart of the French surfing industry and INSIDER TIP▸ one of the first addresses for surfers – because the sea drops away steeply beyond the sand banks, which

FORCE BASQUE

The types of sports that the Basques have kept alive since time immemorial are archaic indeed – tug-of-war *(soka-tira)*, wood chopping *(aizkolariak)*, turning a heavy ox-cart on its own axis *(orga joko)* and stone-lifting *(harri altxatzea)* – and that really does mean lifting: the stones weigh several hundred kilograms. What has its roots in the needs of everyday farming life is today fought

out as part of the *force basque*, strictly regulated competitions among the teams from Basque villages. The best known festival is held in Saint-Palais in August. The traditional Basque ball game – pelota, a kind of Basque version of fives or squash that two teams play against a *fronton*, a high wall – can also be played by those who are not bodybuilders!

results in particularly high waves. Golf, surfing, tennis and cycling are some of the other activities available here. Those who want to practice their surfing skills can do so at the ● École de Surf Aloha (Plage des Bourdaines | tel. 06 99 55 01 96 | www.aloha-ecoledesurf.com).

An elegant country-house ambience is exuded by the lovely Les Hortensias du Lac (18 rooms | 1578, Av. du Tour du Lac | tel. 05 58 43 99 00 | www.hortensias-du-lac.com | Expensive) beside the sea. Just 100 m/328 ft from the sea and 300 m/984 ft from the centre is the friendly little Hôtel La Paloma (18 rooms | 156, Av. de la Côte d'Argent | tel. 05 58 43 46 00 | www.hotel-hossegor-lapaloma.com | Moderate), which also has a pool. Hôtel 202 (22 rooms | 202, Av. du Golf | tel. 05 58 43 22 02 | www.hotel202.fr | Expensive) in the centre of Hossegor is elegant and stylish and close to the golf club in Soorts. Information: 166, Place de la Gare | tel. 05 58 41 79 00 | www.hossegor.fr

ONDRES-PLAGE (142 B4) (𝔐 C16)

The 2 km/1.2 mi-long sandy beach makes Ondres-Plage (pop. 4200) an attractive resort. The culture here is undoubtedly Basque as shown, for example, in the locals' love of pelota. Pine forestry is no longer the most important industry but tourism instead. An excellent fish restaurant with a Spanish accent on the beach is La Plancha du Pêcheur (daily | 37, Impasse Nicolas Brémontier | tel. 08 91 65 87 18 (*) | la-plancha-du-pecheur.zenchef.com | Moderate), a beautifully-run, friendly hotel in a quiet location with a small pool where breakfast is served is Le Lodge (25 rooms | 1180, Av. du 11 Novembre 1918 | tel. 05 59 45 27 02 | www.hotel-le-lodge.com | Moderate) Information: 1750, Av. du 11 Novembre 1918 | tel. 05 59 45 19 19 | www.seignanx-tourisme.com

SAINT-JEAN-DE-LUZ

(142 B5) (𝔐 C16) **10 km/6.2 mi from the Spanish border is the delightful fishing and holiday resort ★ Saint-Jean-de-Luz (pop. 13,000).**

All that remains of this former whaling village is a dozen fishing boats in the harbour. Today its industries are tourism, the surfing industry and exclusive culinary products. The Old Town is tucked away behind the harbour, beyond that is the beach that is protected from the fierce Atlantic by sea walls. The highest waves of the Atlantic have been recorded here just 2 km/1.25 mi from the coast. Surfers are taken out to them on jet skis or even by helicopter.

In 1660, world history was written in Saint-Jean-de-Luz when the Sun King, Louis XIV, married the Spanish Infanta Maria Theresia – an alliance that sealed peace between the two countries after 24 years of war and ensured France's position of supremacy in Europe. Today, the town has almost joined up with Ciboure (pop. 6000) on the left bank of the River Nivelle. There is free parking behind the station.

SIGHTSEEING

PORT

Saint-Jean-de-Luz has always been a wealthy place. The houses on the port were built by prosperous shipowners and their façades are a colourful mixture of styles that testify to the owners' cosmopolitan history. Almost every house has a look-out tower with a view of the harbour from which enemies as well as ships returning home could be spotted.

The church where the Sun King was married deserves a golden altar: Saint-Jean Baptiste

MAISON LOUIS XIV

The monarch spent 40 days in this house built in 1643 in preparation for his wedding. Furniture from the period and an exhibition bring this legendary union and the history of the town to life. *Place Louis XIV | June and Sept/Oct guided tours daily 11am, 3pm, 4pm and 5pm, July/Aug 10.30am–12.30pm and 2.30pm–6.30pm*

PLACE LOUIS XIV

This square exudes the charm of the south with its cafés, bars and music pavilion in the middle. Artists set up their easels in the shade of the plane trees while pastis is sipped in the bars round about. This is also where you'll find the house where the Sun King resided.

SAINT-JEAN-BAPTISTE

The 17th century church with the short octagonal (watch) tower was built for the wedding of the Sun King. Plain and simple on the outside, today it illustrates the town's wealth with, for instance, a gold-plated retable.

FOOD & DRINK

LA BROUILLARTA ⭑

This excellent location, which is situated directly above the beach is matched by the very well-prepared specialities from the sea as well as from the mountains. *Closed Mon/Tue | 48, Promenade Jacques Thibaud | tel. 05 59 51 29 51 | www.restaurant-lebrouillarta.com | Moderate*

LE KAÏKU

Very good fish and lamb dishes in the town's oldest establishment. *Closed Sun/Mon | 17, Rue de la République | tel. 05 59 26 13 20 | Expensive*

CHEZ MARGOT À SOCOA

This restaurant serves authentic Basque cuisine with the focus on seafood. It is located in Ciboure on the other side of the harbour. *Closed July/Aug Wed and Thu lunchtime. | 41, Av. du Commandant Passicot | tel. 05 59 47 18 30 | www.chezmargot.com | Moderate*

LE PEITA

Local specialities ranging from air-dried ham and cheese from the Pyrenees to fish and seafood. *Daily | 21, Rue Pierre-Louis Tourasse | tel. 05 59 26 86 66 | www.restaurant-lepeita.com | Budget*

SHOPPING

There is a daily morning *market* in the ● market halls, and local products are also sold in the surrounding area on Tuesdays and Fridays. Most of the boutiques are on the *Rue Gambetta*. Tablecloths, napkins and fabrics in the typical bright stripes of the Basque are available at *Le Comptoir du Toucan (31, Rue Gambetta)*. Basque hams and salamis are available from *Pierre Oteiza (10, Rue de la République | www.pierreoteiza.com)*, first-class specialities from the region are also available at INSIDER TIP *Aux Provinces Gourmandes (15, Rue du Maréchal Harispe)*. Delightful almond macrons that are said to have been served at the wedding of the Sun King are still made to the same rec-

LOW BUDGET

As befits a meeting place for surfers, Hossegor has various outlet stores for surfer fashions. The Pédebert industrial park is home to one surfing specialist after another, with outlets including e.g. Billabong, Rip Curl and Quiksilver.

You would do well to visit the *Musée Basque et de l'Histoire de Bayonne* in Bayonne on the first Sunday of the month in July and August – admission is free then!

ipe at INSIDER TIP *Maison Adam (6, Rue de la République | www.maisonadam. fr)*. Be sure to try the chocolate-dipped peperoni as well!

SPORTS & ACTIVITIES

All kinds of watersports from jet skiing to surfing rank top in Saint-Jean-de-Luz. Sailing, diving and waterskiing can be learnt in neighbouring Ciboure. Bicycles can be rented at the station. Golf players head for *Golf de Chantaco (Route d'Ascain | tel. 05 59 26 14 22 | www.chantaco.com)*. There is also a *swimming pool* on the *Route d'Ascain*. Pelota can be played at the *Trinquet Anderenia (Quartier Ametzague | tel. 05 59 26 12 12)*. You can book a two-hour introduction (*Mon and Thu, July/Aug also Tue 10am*) through the tourist office. Thalassotherapy: ● *Hélianthal (Place Maurice Ravel | tel. 05 59 51 51 51 | www.thalazur.fr)*

ENTERTAINMENT

There's gambling at the chic *Casino (Place Maurice Ravel)*. A popular meeting place in the evening is the bar *Chez Renauld (4, Blvd. Victor Hugo)* in what was once a car workshop. Many night owls who want to go clubbing do so in Biarritz or INSIDER TIP *Guéthary*, the next place on the way to Biarritz, where the bars and restaurant with sea views are also popular with celebrities, e.g. the *Bar Basque (9, Av. Monseigneur Mugabure)*.

WHERE TO STAY

LES ALMADIES

Charmingly furnished small hotel near the harbour and beach. The lovely wooden terrace is perfect for a sundowner. *7 rooms | 58, Rue Gambetta | tel. 05 59*

85 34 48 | www.hotel-les-almadies.com |
Moderate–Expensive

HÔTEL DE LA PLAGE

The fabulous location on the promenade and very friendly service are
among this hotel's main attractions.
🌿 Some of the rooms have sea views;
Garage. *22 rooms | Promenade Jacques-
Thibaud | tel. 05 59 51 03 44 | www.
hoteldelaplage.com | Moderate*

20, Blvd. Victor Hugo | tel. 05 59 26 03
16 | www.saint-jean-de-luz.com

WHERE TO GO

CORNICHE BASQUE ★ 🌿
(142 A–B5) (*🗺 B–C16*)

South-west of Saint-Jean-de-Luz is where
the Route de la Corniche (D 912) begins,
which runs along the rocky Basque coast
towards the Spanish border. Apart from
the fabulous views of the Atlantic, there
is also plenty of unspoilt coastal landscape to admire.

HENDAYE (142 A5) (*🗺 B16*)

Shortly before the Spanish border and
12 km/7.5 mi west of Saint-Jean-de-Luz is
this lively, if not especially elegant holiday resort (pop. 11,000). Its attractions
include the broad, 3 km/1.9 mi beach
with its moderate (for the area) surf and
several lovely old villas with flower-filled
gardens. Information: *67, Blvd. de la
Mer | tel. 05 59 20 00 34 | www.hendaye-
tourisme.fr*

SARE AND LA RHUNE
(142 B5) (*🗺 C16–17*)

14 km/8.7 mi south of Saint-Jean-de-Luz
is *Sare* (pop. 2200), a quiet Basque village. The *Grottes de Sare (mid April–July*

What an aroma! Freshly-baked almond macrons from Maison Adam

*and Sept daily 10am–6pm, Aug 10am–
7pm, Oct 10am–5pm, Nov/Dec and mid
Feb–mid April Mon–Fri 2pm–5pm, Sat/
Sun 1pm–5pm | www.grottesdesare.fr),*
which were inhabited an amazing
45,000 years ago, are remarkable. Their
story is told in a sound and light show.
Close by, on the Saint-Ignace Pass, is the
station for the *Train de la Rhune (mid
July–Aug daily 8am–5.30pm, April–mid
July and Sept/Oct 9.30am–11.30am and
2pm–4pm every 35 minutes | return
18 euros | www.rhune.com).* This old-
fashioned rack railway spends 30 minutes travelling up the 900 m/2953 ft Py-
renean mountain 🌿 *La Rhune*, the
peak of which is already on Spanish soil.

DISCOVERY TOURS

① FRENCH ATLANTIC COAST AT A GLANCE

START: ❶ Nantes	12 days
END: ⓮ Saint-Jean-de-Luz	driving time (without stops) approx. 14–18 hours
Distance: ➡ approx. 925 km/575 mi	

COSTS: min. 2000 euros for 2 persons (including accommodation in a double room, petrol, entrance fees, hiring costs and all activities, without eating and drinking)

IMPORTANT TIPS: The ferry time table ❼ Phare de Cordouan depends on tides: *www.phare-de-cordouan.fr*; if it leaves too early for you, ferry to the Médoc peninsula – the tour to the lighthouse is also possible from Le-Verdon-sur-Mer. Bicycle hire in every village and many hotels in ❸ Noirmoutier.

Would you like to explore the places that are unique to this region? Then the Discovery Tours are just the thing for you – they include terrific tips for stops worth making, breathtaking places to visit, selected restaurants and fun activities. It's even easier with the Touring App: download the tour with map and route to your smartphone using the QR Code on pages 2/3 or from the website address in the footer below – and you'll never get lost again even when you're offline.

TOURING APP

→ p. 2/3

This tour will take you from Nantes in the north along the coast to Saint-Jean-de-Luz in the Basque province of Labourd. On the way, you'll visit the loveliest islands, sample wines from Bordeaux and experience nature on the land and in the water – sky-high dunes, wide beaches and the surf in the Basque country.

In ➊ Nantes → p. 38 at the castle of the Dukes of Brittany, you'll learn all about the region where world history was written in the Middle Ages. In the evening, treat yourself to a romantic dinner up the river on the Erdre. Next morning, continue on your way to

DAY 1–3
➊ Nantes
69 km/42.9 mi

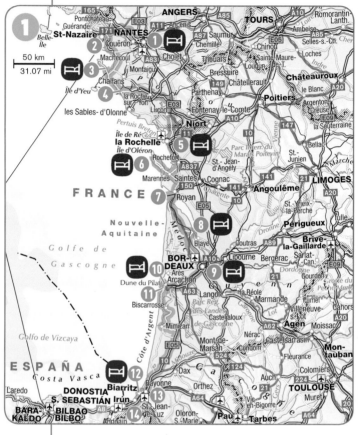

2 Saint-Nazaire → p. 36, where the Loire flows into the Atlantic. Visit the **Escal'Atlantic** museum to experience life on a huge ocean liner of the kind that was once built in Saint-Nazaire. **Then follow the coast** to the **3 Île de Noirmoutier → p. 58**: for cycling, (sun) bathing, seafood consuming, relaxing. Arrange to spend two nights on the island so you experience it at all the tides. Set off on shanks's pony to explore the island for a couple of hours, then go INSIDER TIP land sailing and let yourself be carried along by the wind. You can learn the basics in 1.5 hours at **Sel ton Char** (tel. 06 71 81 00 55 | www. sel-ton-char.fr).

DISCOVERY TOURS

Continue **south along the coast**. In the morning, take a break in the pretty resort of ④ **Saint-Gilles-Croix-de-Vie** → p. 61. Time for a walk along the beach and a bowl of mussels or grilled sardines at **Moulerie de la Gare**. The lively, historic harbour town ⑤ **La Rochelle** → p. 53 is the next stop in your trip. Spend a night at the hotel to explore the buzzing **old town** in the evening, and next day visit the **Aquarium** before continuing your journey to the ⑥ **Île d'Oléron** → p. 46. There, the beaches, pretty little harbours and beautiful landscape provide a wonderful backdrop for two nights on the second-biggest French island in Europe. Try stand-up paddling with **Diabolo Fun** *(Plage des Huttes | Saint-Dénis-d'Oléron | tel. 05 46 47 98 97 | www.diabolofun.com)* to combine exercise and enjoying the countryside – followed in the evening by the famous oysters of Oléron, e.g. at the restaurant **L'Écailler**.

Back on the mainland, drive to Royan and take a boat trip to the ⑦ **Phare de Cordouan** → p. 63. On it, you will find out how the lighthouse keepers worked on this over 400-year-old tower in the middle of the estuary. **Once you have crossed over to the southern shore of the Gironde to the Médoc peninsula, head for** ⑧ **Pauillac** → p. 81, home to some of the world's most famous wine castles. Check into the hotel for a night, then go to the **Maison du Tourisme et du Vin** and book yourself on a wine-tasting session at one of the world-famous estates. Big city flair awaits in ⑨ **Bordeaux** → p. 71. At the **Musée d'Aquitaine** you will find out everything you need to know about the central part of the Atlantic coast, from wine-making and the 100-Year War to art, it has everything that has shaped the region over the past 2000 years. Increase your knowledge of wine in the evening over an excellent tasting menu at the gourmet restaurant **Le Chapon Fin**.

Once you have discovered which is your favourite Bordeaux, the next step in the adventure is all about the ocean: at the traditional seaside resort of ⑩ **Arcachon** → p. 64 you can combine your desire for exercise with relaxation at INSIDER TIP **Paddle Yoga Pilates** with **Surf en Buch**. You'll exercise your whole body and relax your mind in this combination of Pilates and yoga – on a surfboard on the water. **Just outside the town** is the ⑪ **Dune du Pilat** → p. 68, unique natural landscape. Treat

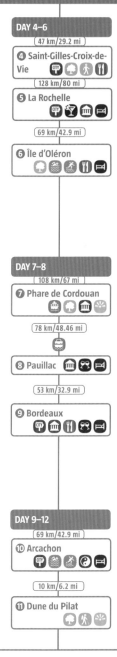

DAY 4–6
47 km/29.2 mi
④ Saint-Gilles-Croix-de-Vie
128 km/80 mi
⑤ La Rochelle
69 km/42.9 mi
⑥ Île d'Oléron

DAY 7–8
108 km/67 mi
⑦ Phare de Cordouan
78 km/48.46 mi
⑧ Pauillac
53 km/32.9 mi
⑨ Bordeaux

DAY 9–12
69 km/42.9 mi
⑩ Arcachon
10 km/6.2 mi
⑪ Dune du Pilat

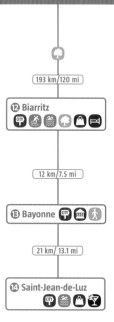

193 km/120 mi

⑫ Biarritz

12 km/7.5 mi

⑬ Bayonne

21 km/13.1 mi

⑭ Saint-Jean-de-Luz

yourself to a little stroll through the dune landscape and enjoy the fabulous views. Next day, follow the Côte d'Argent through the region's characteristic pine forests and into the French Basque region. After the endless beaches of the "Silver Coast", the Côte Basque is winding and rocky, but also has plenty of lovely bays and beaches. Your destination is ⑫ **Biarritz** → p. 84. Spend two nights at this eternally young traditional seaside resort and meeting place for surfers. As well as lovely beaches and high waves, you'll also find a pretty **old town** and excellent shopping. Stroll through the **market hall** in the morning before practising your surfing in the afternoon: the **Hastea** surfing school *(Plage de la Côte des Basques | tel. 06 81 93 98 66 | www.hastea.com)* will soon have you up on your board. Next day, visit nearby ⑬ **Bayonne** → p. 90 and admire the timber-framed houses in the **old town**. On the last day, it's just a stone's throw to the idyllic bathing and fishing resort of ⑭ **Saint-Jean-de-Luz** → p. 92. This is the perfect place to buy all your souvenirs – e.g. tea towels and tablecloths in Basque designs – and raise a glass of pastis to your trip on the sycamore-lined **Place Louis XIV**.

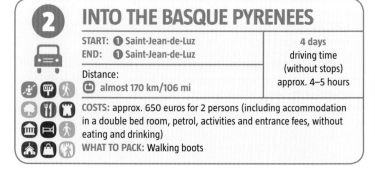

2 INTO THE BASQUE PYRENEES

START: ❶ Saint-Jean-de-Luz
END: ❶ Saint-Jean-de-Luz

4 days
driving time
(without stops)
approx. 4–5 hours

Distance:
🕐 almost 170 km/106 mi

COSTS: approx. 650 euros for 2 persons (including accommodation in a double bed room, petrol, activities and entrance fees, without eating and drinking)

WHAT TO PACK: Walking boots

This tour takes you to the green mountainous hinterland of the Basque coast. Explore the area on foot and by canoe and enjoy the dark chocolate in Bayonne and authentic cuisine in picture-book Basque villages with their white-washed houses and typical red-tiled roofs amidst the green peaks of the mountains

DAY 1

❶ Saint-Jean-de-Luz

4 km/2.5 mi

From ❶ **Saint-Jean-de-Luz take the D 918 towards Ascain.** The village is 6 km/3.7 mi from the coast on the little river Nivelle that is as rapid here as water sports enthusiasts would want. Dreams come true at

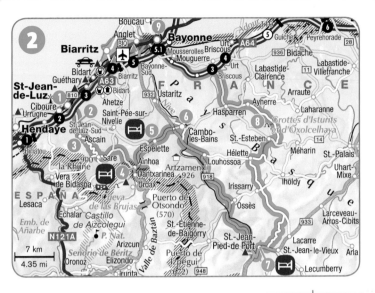

② **Aquabalade** *(July/Aug daily 10am–6pm, otherwise book in advance | tel. 06 62 58 09 97 | www.aquabalade. com)* **at a bend in the river:** hire a canoe at this canoe and stand-up paddling hire centre, and experience the river up close! Stop for photos at **③** **Ascain**. There is a restored **Roman bridge** over the river here, and the medieval church is also lovely. **Continue along the D 4 past Sare to arrive at ④ Ainhoa**, which has officially been named one of the prettiest villages in France. Its history as a milestone for pilgrims on the Route to Santiago goes back to the 12th century. The **fronton**, the typical walled pelota court, is as much a part of this Basque idyll as the five-storey **bell tower** and the chapel of **Notre-Dame d'Aranzazu** with gold-plated wood carvings. In the evening, sample the Basque specialities at the restaurant **Ithurria** *(mid Aug– June closed Thu noon and Wed | Place du Fronton | tel. 05 59 29 92 11 | www.ithurria.com | Moderate–Expensive)*. Conveniently, this excellent establishment in a restored inn for pilgrims also has 28 hotel rooms.

In the morning take the D 20 to ⑤ Espelette. Have a quieter day today, because there's going to be another hike tomorrow. The red peppers that hang drying from all the walls in autumn make this little town one of the most popular photo motifs in the region – as well as a wonder-

② Aquabalade

1 km/0.6 mi

③ Ascain

17 km/10.6 mi

④ Ainhoa

DAY 2

11 km/6.8 mi

⑤ Espelette

ful stage finish. Enjoy a long stroll through the streets and spice shops. At the **Syndicat du Piment d'Espelette** (Mon–Fri 9am–1pm and 2pm–6pm | www.pimentdespelette.com) you'll find all you want to know about the properties of and uses for the fresh and dried peppers. You can taste and buy hot and mild pastes and products e.g. at the **Boutique of producer Bipertegia** (Place Jeu de Paume). Spend the night at the Basque-style hotel **Euzkadi** (27 rooms | 285, Karrika Nagusia | tel. 05 59 93 91 88 | www.hotel-restaurant-euzkadi.com | Moderate), which also has a restaurant (closed Mon/Tue).

DAY 3

7 km/4.4 mi

6 Cambo-les-Bains
🚶 🛏 ☕ 🍴 🏛

40 km/24.9 mi

7 Saint-Jean-Pied-de-Port
🍽 🛏 🚶 🛍 🚌

6 Cambo-les-Bains, a traditional spa resort with an upper and lower part, is **just a few kilometres past Espelette**. As well as thermal spas, it also contains a network of 60 hiking trails of various lengths and levels of difficulty (short.travel/fra6). The tourism office (OT) offers a 6-km/3.7-mi hike (Wed/Fri 9am–12.45pm from OT | To book tel. 05 59 29 70 25) on which you will be able observe vultures. Lunch will be served by "Tante Ursula", at whose **Auberge Chez Tante Ursule** (daily | Fronton du Bas-Cambo | tel. 05 59 29 78 23 | www.auberge-tante-ursule.com | Budget) the menu always includes a Basque speciality as the dish of the day. In the afternoon, visit the magnificent **Villa Arnaga** (2, Route du Docteur Camino | July/Aug daily 10am–7pm, April–June and Sept–mid Oct 9.30am–12.30pm and 2pm–6pm, otherwise book in advance on tel. 05 59 29 83 92 | www.arnaga.com) built by Edmon Rostand, the author of "Cyrano de Bergerac", which includes a library, paintings and a lovely garden. **30 km/18.6 mi along the D 918 and up into the Pyrenees, you'll come to today's destination of 7 Saint-Jean-Pied-de-Port**, a lovely little town 8 km/5 mi from the Spanish border, and the final stopping point on the Route to Santiago off pass road to Roncesvalles in Spain. Walk up to the **citadel** and around the fortress walls, admiring the views of the vineyards, valleys and the surrounding Basque Country. There are lovely shops along the cobblestoned **Rue de la Citadelle**. Pop in to the **Boutique du Pèlerin** (32, Rue de la Citadelle), which has hiking equipment and literature on the Route to Santiago as well as lovely souvenirs. For a stylish night's sleep, check in to the hotel **Les Pyrénées** (14 rooms | 19, Place du Général de Gaulle | tel. 05 59 37 01 01 | www.hotel-les-pyrenees.com | Expensive) with a gourmet restaurant (closed Mon evening and Tue, Basque cuisine) and pool.

Signature feature of the Basque Pyrenees – the *piment d'Espelette*

A double highlight awaits you on the last day: stalactite caves and ancient rock engravings. **Take the Route Impériale des Cimes (D 22) towards the coast.** Just before Hasparren turn right to the ❽ **Grottes d'Isturitz et d'Oxocelhaya** *(July/Aug daily 10am–6pm, June and Sept daily guided tours 10.30am, 11.30am and 2pm–5pm, mid March–May and Oct–mid Nov 2pm–5pm | www.grottes-isturitz.com)*: the latter contain stalactite formations, while Isturitz has ancient rock engravings. **It's then a good 30 km/18.6 mi to ❾ Bayonne → p. 90,** where at the **Atelier du Chocolat** you can take a look behind the scenes at the chocolate "laboratory" and learn all about the production of these delicious calorie bombs – tasting included, of course. **Another 20 km/12.4 mi, and you'll be back at ❶ Saint-Jean-de-Luz.**

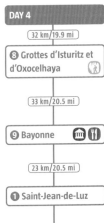

DAY 4

32 km/19.9 mi

❽ Grottes d'Isturitz et d'Oxocelhaya

33 km/20.5 mi

❾ Bayonne

23 km/20.5 mi

❶ Saint-Jean-de-Luz

103

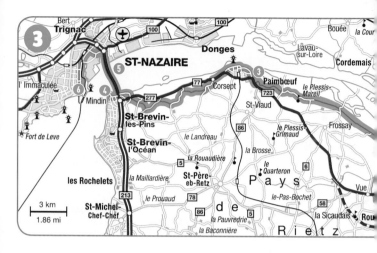

ARTS, CANALS, OCEAN CRUISERS: CYCLING ALONG THE LOIRE ESTUARY

START: ① Nantes
END: ⑥ Escal'Atlantic

Distance:
➡ almost 70 km/43.5 mi

1 day
driving time
(without stops)
approx. 5–6 hours

COSTS: Hire bike 15 (e-bike 30) euros, entrance fee ⑥ Escal'Atlantic 13 euros, possibly 9 euros for the train, plus eating and drinking

IMPORTANT TIPS: Bicycle hire: *Détours de Loire (Allée de la Maison Rouge, 800 m/2627 ft from the train station | tel. 02 40 48 75 37 | www.detoursdeloire.com)* From Saint-Nazaire back to Nantes it will take about 30–40 minutes by train. You won't have to pay agio for the bicycle in local trains.

From the heart of Nantes, cycle along the Loire to its estuary. Along the way you will see and experience how the former industrial region has become an exciting art and cultural landscape. At the end of the tour in Saint-Nazaire, follow in the footsteps of the ocean giants that were once built here.

① Nantes
23 km/14.3 mi

10:00am The tour begins at the station in ① Nantes → p. 38. The cycle path starts out heading west along the northern bank of the Loire, through the old harbour and Chantenay. **In Couëron use the *bac*, the Loire shuttle**

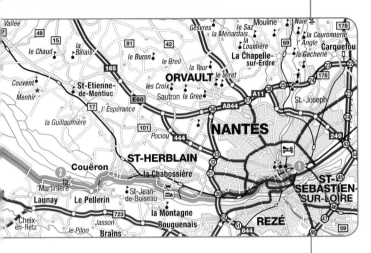

(free), to cross to the southern bank and Le Pellerin. Follow the left bank to the ➋ **Canal de la Martinière**. This waterway was constructed in the 19th century to enable larger ships access to Nantes – because of the sand banks, the Loire was frequently impassable for heavy ships between Paimbœuf and Le Pellerin. Opened in 1892, the canal was already abandoned in the early 20th century. Today it is used to control the water in the region's wetlands, and is once again an idyllic part of the natural landscape. Just where it flows into the Loire, the sailboat installation **'Misconceivable'** by the Austrian artist Erwin Wurm leans over the quay wall – an exhibition of the INSIDER TIP culture project Estuaire *(www.estuaire.info)*, which was started in 2007 to add new life to the former industrial area. Today there are over two dozen installations in the area of the Loire estuary between Nantes and Saint-Nazaire – an amazing open-air museum.

12:00pm Follow the canal at your own pace to ➌ **PaimbSuf**. Here you will see the accessible work of art **Le Jardin Étoilé** by Kinya Maruyama, which is also part of the Estuaire project. Fortify yourself with a delicious, typically Breton galette *(buckwheat pancake with savoury fillings)* at the crêperie **L'Estuaire** *(closed Mon and evenings except Fri–Sun | Chemin de l'Estuaire | tel. 02 44 06 20 42 | restaurantcreperielestuaire.fr | Budget)*. **Another 12 km/ 7.5 mi, and you'll arrive at Saint-Brévin-les-Pins.** Watch

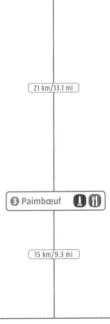

➋ Canal de la Martinière

21 km / 13.1 mi

➌ Paimbœuf

15 km / 9.3 mi

❹ "Serpent d'Océan" ⓘ

3 km/1.9 mi

❺ Pont de Saint-Nazaire 🏛 ✳

7 km/4.4 mi

❻ Escal'Atlantic 🏛

out here for the sea serpent ❹ **"Serpent d'Océan"** by the Chinese artist Huang Yong Ping, where the waves break over this 130 m/427 ft long skeleton when the tide is in.

03:30pm Now comes the most spectacular part of the tour: **on the bridge ❺ Pont de Saint-Nazaire which has an inclination of 5.6 percent you'll cross the Loire estuary.** Although you can cycle over the bridge, there is no separate cycle path. So the traffic (and the wind!) may spoil your enjoyment somewhat, but the views will certain compensate for that at least in part. **At the end, turn left onto Blvd. Paul Leferme (D 971),** which will take you to the ❻ **Escal'Atlantic** → p. 36. A circular tour on board this spectacular museum in what was once a submarine bunker is an impressive end to the tour: it is designed like one of the ocean cruisers that used to be built here.

Start your ride around the Bassin d'Arcachon in Cap Ferret

4 BIKING AND BATHING AT THE BASSIN D'ARCACHON

START: ❶ Arcachon END: ❶ Arcachon	1 day driving time (without stops) approx. 6 hours
Distance: 🚲 approx. 75 km/46.6 mi	

COSTS: ferry 7.50 euros per person, bicycle 6 euros, oyster museum Maison de l'Huître 5.80 euros, bird reserve ❹ Réserve Ornithologique du Teich 8.90 euros

WHAT TO PACK: Drinking water, sun protection, bathing gear, spyglass if necessary

IMPORTANT TIPS: Bicycle hire (also e-bikes) in many hotels and at numerous bicycle hiring station, e.g. Dingo Vélos *(1, Rue Grenier | tel. 05 56 83 44 09 | www.dingo-velo.com)*

This tour once around the Bassin d'Arcachon offers plenty of variety and wonderful panoramas. It takes you through salt meadows and to an oyster farm, so the focus is on the landscape and nature. At 75 km/46.6 mi, it is ideal both for experienced cyclists and for e-bikers.

10:00am The starting point is the Thiers jetty in ❶ Arcachon → p. 64. In order to cycle all around the bay, **take the boat from here** *(www.bateliers-arcachon.com)* at **10am: line 1 will get you to** ❷ Cap Ferret → p. 68 in 30 minutes. On your arrival, the headland and lighthouse will be to your left. And your visit starts with lovely views of the sand bank at Arguin. More athletic visitors will get their pulses racing by climbing up the 52 m/170.6 ft high lighthouse Phare du Cap Ferret – and their reward will be the fabulous views as far as the dunes of Pilat! **Then head north on the D 106**, past the oyster banks and with views of the Île-aux-Oiseaux in the Basin of Arcachon. **Via Arès at the northern end of the Basin**, the route will take you through salt meadows and on to the **lively resorts of Andernos-les-Bains** and ❸ Lanton. Park your bikes at the lovely Plage de Taussat and relax on the beach.

01:30pm Lunch of mussels, salad or tapas is at Moule & Co *(daily | 1, Place de Courcy Taussat | tel. 05 56 26 47 36 | www.restaurant-moulesandco-taussat.fr | Budget)*. **Afterwards, set off for Audenge.** It gets a little quieter

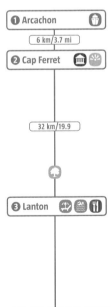

now. Seagulls and count-
less other bird calls greet
you as you approach the
bird reserve **④ Réserve
Ornithologique du Teich**
*(July/Aug daily 10am–
9pm, mid April–June and
first half of Sept 10am–
7pm, mid Sept–mid April
10am–6pm | www.reser
ve-ornithologique-du-
teich.com)*, which is ac-
cessible to cyclists.

04:00pm In **⑤ Gujan-
Mestras** it becomes more
urban again. In the self-
proclaimed oyster farm-
ing capital – more than

half the oysters grown in the bay come from here – you
can inform yourself about all aspects of oyster cultivation
in the **Maison de l'Huître** *(June–Aug daily, Sept–May
Mon–Sat 10am–12.30pm and 2.30pm–6pm | Port de Lar-
ros | www.maisondelhuitre.fr)*. And now on to neigbour-
ing **Les Pavois** *(closed Mon except July/Aug | 113, Port de*

---

21 km/13.1 mi

**④ Réserve Ornitho-
logique du Teich**

5 km/3.1 mi

⑤ Gujan-Mestras

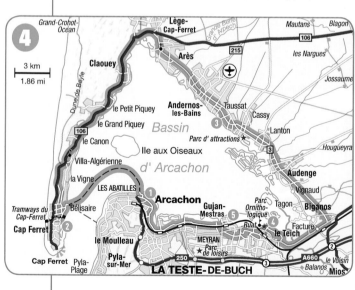

A stop at the beach is a guaranteed carrot for any cycling tour on Noirmoutier

Larros | tel. 05 56 66 38 71 | www.restaurant-lespavois. com | Budget) – after all, we know you want to try the seafood as well! **The final leg takes you from Gujan back to ① Arcachon** → p. 64.

12 km/7.5 mi

① Arcachon

5 BEACHES, OYSTERS AND SALT PONDS ON NOIRMOUTIERS

START: ① L'Herbaudière END: ① L'Herbaudière	1 day driving time (without stops) approx. 4 hours
Distance: 🚲 almost 50 km/31.1 mi	

COSTS: approx. 45 euros per person (including hire bike, entrance fees, lunch and oyster tasting)
WHAT TO PACK: Drinking water, sun protection, bathing gear

IMPORTANT TIPS: Bicycles are ubiquitous on Noirmoutier – also hire bikes. Almost all hotels and many shops hire bicycles. A perfect day for this tour is Wednesday as it is the market day in ③ Barbâtre.

The flat Île de Noirmoutier → p. 58 is perfect for cycling. Almost 80 km/49.7 mi are signposted cycle paths, and take you – some asphalted, some firm sand paths – through salt evaporation ponds, forests, small towns and along the sea.

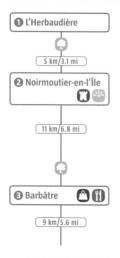

❶ L'Herbaudière

5 km/3.1 mi

❷ Noirmoutier-en-l'Île

11 km/6.8 mi

❸ Barbâtre

9 km/5.6 mi

10:00am Set off from the sport harbour of ❶ L'Herbaudière. **Head for the D 5 via the Rue du Port.** To your left are fields, to your right the salt ponds where *fleur de sel* is laboriously obtained. After about 20 minutes you'll arrive at the island's capital of ❷ Noirmoutier-en-l'Île. You can't miss the beautifully preserved **castle**, which was built in the 12th century to defend the island. Take an hour to walk around, and enjoy the lovely view of the island and the Baie de Bourgneuf from the tower. **Cycle 4 km/2.5 mi parallel to the D 948 to La Guérinière.** This is where the island's narrowest point starts: you cycle between the Atlantic on the right and the calmer Baie de Bourgneuf on the left until you see ❸ Barbâtre ahead of you. On Wednesdays there is a lovely **market** on the Place du Marché. Treat yourself to sweet cherries and fragrant peaches for a beach picnic in the afternoon! You'll also find plenty at **La Paillotte**

A sea breeze for your mouth and stomach – a dozen oysters directly from the farmer

du Gois: as well as fresh fruit, it also sells regional products such as salt, jams and wine.

`12:30pm` Feeling hungry? The pizzeria **La Mano Negra** *(closed Wed except Jul/ Aug | 6, Route du Gois | tel. 02 52 39 89 55 | Budget)* serves delicious `INSIDER TIP` pizzas with regional toppings such as seafood, Vendée ham and Roquefort. **Travel south for another 20 minutes along the D 95 and you'll come to ❹ Pointe de la Fosse**, the southern tip of the island: time for some photos! If you want to swim, head right and find your perfect spot on the beach.

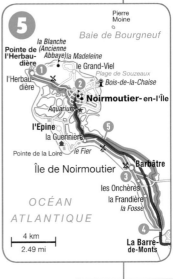

`04:00pm` Now it's time to pour the sand out of your shoes and get back on the saddle. **The Rue de la Pointe takes you to a roundabout, where you turn right onto a bike-friendly sandy path. After about 45 minutes, you'll arrive at the Port du Bonhomme.** In the harbour on the terrace of the oyster producer ❺ **La Godaille** you can enjoy a plate of twelve oysters and a glass of white wine for an extremely reasonable 10 euros. **Take the cycle path to Noirmoutier-en-l'Île** and cycle through the salt evaporation ponds for a further 20 minutes, and you'll be back at ❶ **L'Herbaudière**.

❹ Pointe de la Fosse

12 km/7.5 mi

❺ La Godaille

12 km/7.5 mi

❶ L'Herbaudière

SPORTS & ACTIVITIES

You certainly won't get bored here! Sport is just as much part of the French Atlantic Coast's tourist capital as its wide beaches.

An excellent infrastructure for all forms of watersport awaits you on the inland lakes and the Côte d'Argent. On top of this, there is a well established network of cycle paths and bridleways and masses of golf courses.

CANOE & KAYAK TRIPS

Canoe and kayak trips are available on the sea, rivers and lakes. The quality seal of approval 'Point Canoë Nature' awarded by the *Fédération Française de Canoë Kayak (www.ffck.org)* is an indication of a private company's high standards. The Bassin d'Arcachon, the Lac d'Hourtin et de Carcans, the Lac de Lacanau and the Lac de Cazaux et de Sanguinet are ideal for both canoe and kayak trips.

CYCLING

The generally flat Atlantic coast is perfect for cycle tours. Over the past few years, bike touring facilities have been expanded greatly in southwest France. There are around 2000 km/1250 mi of cycle paths between Biscarrosse and Ondres near Capbreton alone and 1000 km/620 mi in the Vendée with more than 70 way-marked tours. It is now possible to cycle the whole way from Brittany to Hendaye on the Spanish border without a break on dedicated paths. The

With plenty of wind and waves the only thing to stop you being permanently on the move on the Atlantic coast is your time

1200 km/750 mi) route runs the length of the Atlantic coast and forms the longest bike path in France and constitutes the French section of the European cycle network Eurovélo 1. Shorter routes, such as the 112 km/70 mi-long *Vélocéan* between Piriac-sur-Mer and Les Moutiers-en-Retz that passes through a lovely stretch of countryside, are also well maintained and signposted.

You can rent bikes virtually everywhere. *Créon*, 25 km/15.5 mi to the southeast of Bordeaux in Entre-Deux-Mers, is unique in France having the very first 'bike station' *(www.lepointrelaisvelo-creon.fr)* You can hire all the equipment there, as you would at a ski station. The map "Cycling tourism in the Aquitaine" is available for download on the website of the Comité Régional de Tourisme d'Aquitaine *(www.tourisme-aquitaine.fr)*. Tips and suggested routes for tours in the Vendée can be found under *www.velo-loisirs.fr*. High-visibility vests with reflectors must be worn at night and in bad weather outside built-up areas.

DIVING

The undersea world off the rocky Côte Basque is especially interesting. Diving schools can also be found further to the north along the Atlantic coast, such as in La Baule, Arcachon and Biscarrosse.

FISHING

In the peak season, fishing from the beach or cliffs is not allowed in many resorts. The inland lakes, canals and rivers are ideal for freshwater fishing. Sea fishing trips are available from a number of harbours on the coast. A fishing permit is only required for the inland lakes, and costs 6–10 euros for a day, 32 euros for a week *(order online at www.cartedepeche.fr)*. General information on fishing spots and licences is available from the *Fédération Française des Pêcheurs en Mer (tel. 04 91 85 19 67 | www.ffpm-national.com)*. Maps and information online: *www.federationpeche.fr*

GOLF

Golf is a traditional sport especially on the Basque coast. The second oldest golf course in France is *Golf de Biarritz Le Phare (www.golfbiarritz.com)*. But there is no shortage of beautiful greens elsewhere, especially in and around Biarritz where there are 10 to choose from. Beginners' courses are available at 5 schools in the *Centre International d'Entraînement au Golf d'Ilbarritz (Av. du Château | tel. 05 59 43 81 30 | www. golf-ilbarritz.com)* in *Bidart* on the cliffs.

HIKING

When hiking, you can experience the area's greatest attractions – the coast and the marshlands – that much more intensely, especially in the nature reserves on the Côte de Lumière. Such routes include those through the Marais de l'Eguille or the Forêt Domanial on Oléron (waymarked routes) or opposite, on the mainland, **INSIDER TIP** through the Bourcefranc-le-Chapus oyster farming region.

LAND YACHTING

At low tide the wide beaches down the Atlantic coast provide perfect conditions for land yachting. One hotspot is *Notre-Dame-de-Monts (www.polenautique.org)* with its almost 30 km/19 mi of beach. The 3-wheeled vehicles with sails *(chars à voile)* can be hired at yachting schools.

RAFTING

Whitewater tours on rubber dinghies are available on rivers in the Pyrenees in the Basque Country in particular. Information from the *Ligue d'Aquitaine de Canoë-Kayak (tel. 05 40 05 01 31)*. Tours on the Nive are offered from Itxassou *Évasion 64 (Maison Errola | tel. 05 59 29 31 69 | www. evasion64.fr)*, for example.

RIDING

Whether along the beach, through salt-marshes, vineyards or in the Pyrenees, there are 8500 km/5300 mi of way-marked bridleways to choose from. Hacks and excursions lasting several days are available. Information and addresses can be obtained from the Comité Régional de Equestre d'Aquitaine *(www.cheval-aquitaine.com)*.

SAILING

Sailing schools and boat rental companies are ten a penny. The tourist information office in each resort has a list of addresses. The French sailing association has given certain seaside resorts a quality seal of approval – the 'Station voile' (e.g. *La Teste-de-Buch, Arcachon* and *Hendaye*). The 'France Station Nautique' label is a guarantee for an extensive range of watersports which always includes sailing.

STAND-UP-PADDLING

This trendy sport is also extremely popular in France. Offers e.g. at *Surf en Pays de Buch (tel. 06 80 05 46 95 | www.ecole desurf-arcachon.com)*. It is also practised on rivers in the hinterland, in Périgord for instance on the Dordogne: *Sup-Périgord (Le Couderc | Cénac-et-Saint-Julien | www. sup-perigord.com)*

SURFING & WINDSURFING

The French Atlantic Coast is one of the world's hotspots for surfing, especial-ly Hossegor and Biarritz. A list of clubs that belong to the French surfing association can be found under *www.surf ingaquitaine.com*. For general information see: *Fédération Française de Surf (tel. 05 58 43 55 88 | www.surfing france.com)*.

The inland lakes are ideal places for windsurfing. Most sailing schools rent out equipment too.

THALASSOTHERAPY

Thalassotherapy, which combines wellness with seawater-based beauty and health treatments, is typical of the Atlantic coast. For this reason thalassotherapy centres are always located beside the sea – and generally they are to be found in a pleasant hotel where a bathrobe becomes your usual holiday wear in a heartbeat.

From Brittany to Spain? If you've got the time, you can even cycle it!

TRAVEL WITH KIDS

France caters well for children (and their parents) in everyday life and on holiday – be it child minding or entertainment, and restaurants have highchairs and cheap *menus enfants* for families.

In most seaside resorts the question 'What can I do?' is easily answered: 'Mickey Club!' The "Clubs de Plage Mickey" *(www.fncp.fr)* offer supervised play and sports on the beach for children aged 3 to 14 years.

Particularly family-friendly accommodation, facilities and events have been given the 'Famille plus' award. Things on offer include surfing, sailing and canoeing especially tailored to children's needs. Many places on the Atlantic are near an inland lake that is safer to swim in.

CÔTE D'AMOUR

LES MACHINES DE L'ÎLE IN NANTES
(136 C3) *(㎠ C4)*

This innovative project offers entertainment for the whole family in the old docklands in Nantes. Mechanical sea and mythical creatures can be mounted on a merry-go-round. A real highlight are the trips on a reeling boat, which involves being sprayed with water. It's also great fun to ride on the 12-m/39.4 ft high *Grand Éléphant. Blvd. Léon Bureau | heavily staggered times see website, main time daily 2pm–5pm, April–Oct 10am–5pm/6pm/7pm | Admission and elephant ride 8.50 euros each, for children (4–17 years) 6.90 euros | www.lesmachines-nantes.fr*

Photo: Beach on the Île de Ré at low tide

Water, sand, lots of amusement parks and an "elephant ride" in Nantes: children will have a real good time here

PIRIAC AVENTURE IN PIRIAC
(136 A2) (*A3*)

Tree canopy adventure for children aged 4+ along various different routes. Also for parents. Hanging from a wire rope or clambering through pipes and across bridges – but always safely harnessed. The adventure park is found in Piriac (*Route de Mesquer*), in Pornic (*www.pornic-aventure.com*) and in Guérande (*www.presquile-aventure.com*). July/Aug daily 9.30am–7.30pm, April–June Wed 1pm–7pm, Sat/Sun 10am–7pm, Sept/Oct Wed, Sat, Sun 1pm–7pm | 21 euros, children depending on age 15/17/19 euros | piriac-aventure.com

PLANÈTE SAUVAGE IN PORT SAINT-PÈRE
(136 C3) (*C4*)

This extensive animal reserve has a 10 km/6.25 mi drive-through safari route where you can see animals from 5 continents. Sea lions perform tricks in the Cité Marine and in the village there is a flamingo island, a monkey forest and a reptile house. *La Chevalerie | Mid July–Aug daily 9.30am–7.30pm, March–mid July and Sept–Nov with occasional days closed 10am–6/7pm | various rates starting at 2 euros | www.planetesauvage.com*

CÔTE DE LUMIÈRE

AQUARIUM IN LA ROCHELLE
(138 B2–3) (*Ⓜ D7*)

Fascinating aquarium with masses of different sea creatures to see – all presented perfectly with young visitors in mind. The fish tanks are at the right height for a child and a trip in the 'lift' puts everyone in the right mood: water shoots up behind the glass walls as if you were really going down to the bottom of the sea. *Bassin des Grands Yachts | July/Aug daily 9am–11pm, April–June and Sept 9am–8pm, Oct–March 10am–8pm | 16 euros, children (aged 3–17) 12 euros | www.aquarium-larochelle.com*

CENTRE AQUATIQUE IN CHÂTELAILLON-PLAGE
(138 B–C3) (*Ⓜ D7*)

Water park with slides, several pools and a water temperature of 29 °C (84.2 °F). *RN137 | July/Aug Mon–Fri 10am–8pm, Sat 11.15pm–8pm, Sun 9am–8pm, times vary other months | 5.50 euros, children (aged 3–16) 4 euros | www.centre-aquatique.com*

L'ÎLE AUX PAPILLONS ON NOIRMOUTIER
(136 B4) (*Ⓜ B4*)

Exotic butterflies from Guyana, Kenya, Madagascar and the Philippines in a jungle environment. *5, Rue de la Fassonière | La Guérinière | June–Aug daily 10am–7.30pm, April/May Mon–Fri 2pm–7pm, Sat/Sun 10.30am–7pm, Sept daily 2pm–7pm | 8.60 euros, children (aged 3–12) 6.30 euros | www.ile-aux-papillons.com*

INSIDER TIP ▶ JARDIN DU VENT IN NOTRE-DAME-DE-MONTS
(136 B4) (*Ⓜ B5*)

(Hands-on) devices in this wonderful open-air display let you see, hear and feel the wind which blows continuously in the Vendée. The wind makes music, blows bubbles and envelops visitors in a scented cloud. *29, Rue Gilbert Cesbron | June–Aug Mon–Fri 10am–7pm, Sat/Sun 2pm–7pm, April/May and Sept Mon–Fri 10am–noon and 2pm–6pm, Sat/Sun 2pm–6pm | 4 euros, children (aged 6–18) 2.20 euros | www.jardinduvent.fr*

ZOO DE LA PALMYRE
(138 B4) (*Ⓜ D9*)

Aminals from 5 continents, including tigers, leopards, giraffes, kangaroos and polar bears can be seen here in large enclosures that give the animals as much freedom as possible. *Av. de Royan | La Palmyre | April–Sept daily 9am–7pm, Oct–March 9am–6pm | 17 euros, children (aged 3–12) 13 euros | www.zoo-palmyre.fr*

CÔTE D'ARGENT

LA HUME IN THE BASSIN D'ARCACHON
(140 A4) (*Ⓜ D12*)

No fewer than five parks in one spot: *Aqualand*, the zoo *La Coccinelle* with over 800 animals, a climbing park, mini golf and *Kid Parc*, with a world scaled down to child size. *La Hume | June–Sept daily 10am–6pm | per park 11–20 euros*

PARC DE L'AVENTURE IN MONTALIVET
(138 B6) (*Ⓜ D10*)

Play at being Tarzan (while safely hooked on in a harness) in the treetops. There is an 'Explorer Route' (min. height 1.10 m/3.6 ft) and an 'Adventurer

Route' (1.4 m/4.6 ft). *Lède de Montalivet | July/Aug daily 10am–8pm, April–June and Sept/Oct Sat 2pm–6pm, Sun 2pm–5.45pm | depending on route 18–20 euros, children taller than 1.4 m/4.6 ft 18 euros, from 1.1 m/3.6 ft or 5 years 14 euros, up to 5 years 8.50 euros | www.laforet-aventure.com*

PORT MINI IN SOUSTONS
(142 C3–4) (*ω C–D15*)
Play at being captain of a Mississippi paddle steamer or explore the seas on the historic sailing ship – the 'Mayflower' – on the Lac de Soustons. Suitable for children aged 9+. The boats can take up to 5 people. *July/Aug Mon–Fri 11am–7pm, Sat/Sun 4pm–7pm, April–June and Sept Wed–Sun 2pm–6pm | 5 euros per person per 15 minutes | www.loisirs-soustons.com*

ZOO DU BASSIN D'ARCACHON IN LA TESTE
(140 A4) (*ω D12*)
One of the largest zoos in France covering 24 acres of forest land near Arcachon. Including pets' corner where the animals can be stroked. *Route de Cazaux | La Teste-de-Buch | 1st half of April and 2nd half of Sept daily 2pm–6.30pm, mid April–mid Sept daily 10am–7pm, Oct–mid Nov Wed, Sat, Sun 2pm–6.30pm | 16 euros, children (aged 2–12) 12 euros | www.zoodubassindarcachon.com*

CÔTE BASQUE

BIARRITZ AQUARIUM
(142 B5) (*ω C16*)
A perfect destination for the whole family with several thousand species and modern, interactive displays. Older children will also love the adjoining Cité de la Mer. *Esplanade du Rocher de la Vierge, staggered opening hours, see website, April–Oct daily 9.30am–8pm | 14.50 euros, children (aged 4–16) 9.80 euros, combined ticket with Cité de la Mer 18.50 euros, children 13 euros | www.aquariumbiarritz.com*

There are 20 different types of shark alone at La Rochelle aquarium

FESTIVALS & EVENTS

FEBRUARY

La Folle Journée de Nantes: This is the name of a series of classical concerts that take place in and around Nantes in the first week of February. *www.folle journee.fr*

MARCH

The international surfing community meets in Biarritz at the end of March for the *Maïder Arostéguy Championship*. *biarritzmaiderarosteguy.fr*

MAY/JUNE

On the weekend after Ascension Day, the Guild of *chocolatiers* in Bayonne invites people to the *Journées du Chocolat* – plenty of opportunities to sample first-rate chocolates.

Saint-Gilles-Croix-de-Vie in the Vendée is the setting for the international jazz festival Saint Jazz sur Vie on Whitsun weekend *www.saint-jazz-sur-vie.com*

JUNE

The vintners announce the quality of the new wine at the *Fête du Printemps* with costume parade in Bordeaux on the third Sunday in June.

On the third Sunday in June, around 1000 marathon runners – and twice as many visitors – gather in the village of Coulon for the *Maraisthon* in Marais Poitevin. Two hiking routes, one of 10 km/6.2 mi and the other 11 km/6.8 mi, are signposted as alternatives. *www.maraisthon.fr*

Bordeaux always invites people to the *Bordeaux Fête le Vin* in even years. *www.bordeaux-fete-le-vin.com*

JULY

Young and established artists and orchestras participate in the INSIDER TIP *Musique au Cœur du Médoc* event in châteaux and monasteries in Médoc – followed by wine tasting. *www.musique aucoeurdumedoc.com.*

At the INSIDER TIP *Biarritz International Groove Festival BIG* the town becomes the meeting place for the electronic music scene in the middle of July. *bigfest.fr*

Fête du Thon (2nd weekend) in Saint-Jean-de-Luz with street music and tuna specialities.

On *Bastille Day* (14 July), the French national day, celebrations – usually starting the evening before – are everywhere. Big fireworks displays.

Fête de la Sardine in La Turballe (mid July and mid August).

Bataille de Castillon in Castillon-la-Bataille. Re-enactment of the battle between England and France that ended the 100 Years' War in 1453 and the British occupation. *www.batailledecastillon.com*

At the end of July/beginning of August, Saint-Nazaire spends two days celebrating the world music festival **Les Escales**.

AUGUST

On the first or second weekend, over 140 wooden sailing boats gather for the **Régates du Bois de la Chaise** off Noirmoutier.

At the **Force Basque** festival of Basque rural sports in the middle of August in Saint-Palais, strong men compete against each other in tug-of-war, wood chopping and stone lifting. *www.force basquesaintpalais.com*

In the middle of August Arcachon celebrates a **Fête de la Mer** with fireworks, lots of music and a huge picnic on the beach.

A giant fireworks display is also staged at the **Nuit Féerique** in Biarritz.

The jazz and world music festival **Les Rendezvous de l'Erdre** in Nantes takes place over four days at the end of August on several stages on the banks of the Erdre. *www.rendezvouserdre.com*

SEPTEMBER

7000 mostly costumed runners take place in the **Médoc-Marathon** on the second weekend in September. *www.mara thondumedoc.com*

In the first half of September, Biarritz is the setting for the festival of ballet **Le Temps d'Aimer la Danse**. *letemps-daimer.com*

PUBLIC HOLIDAYS

1 Jan	*Jour de l'An*
March/April	Easter Monday
	(Lundi de Pâques)
1 May	*Fête du Travail*
8 May	End of WWII in 1945
May/June	*(Ascension Day)*;
	Whit Monday
	(Lundi de Pentecôte)
14 July	*Fête Nationale*
15 Aug	*Assomption*
1 Nov	*Toussaint*
11 Nov	End of WWI in 1918
25 Dec	*Noël*

LINKS, BLOGS, APPS & MORE

www.thalassocotebasque.com Information and addresses – sadly only in French – on thalassotherapy on the Basque coast

www.lesfillesenespadrilles.com Lots of up-to-date tips, addresses and events on this blog (in French), which also contains plenty of information on the attitudes and lifestyles of young women in the Basque Country

www.expat-blog.com/en/directory/europe/france All sorts of weird and wonderful things can happen when living in a foreign country. Just read the blogs of those who have settled in Bordeaux and Nantes!

www.flickr.com/photos/tourisme-aquitaine Photos of the French Atlantic Coast to whet your appetite for more

www.gites-de-france-landes.com, www.gites-sud-atlantique.com Masses of addresses for those looking for that perfect holiday cottage

twitter.com/#!/so_biarritz Pining for the southwest corner of France? Under @SO_Biarritz you can find out up-to-the-minute information from this beautiful town in the Basque Country – from the weather to events, dates of concerts, etc. and what makes the people of Biarritz tick

www.mes3jours.com Everything that occupies people – women in particular – on the Basque coast, and lots of gastronomy tips on Biarritz and the surrounding area in this (French) blog

twitter.com/atout_france_de The French tourism centre is constantly collating and sending out information on tourism, culture and sports in order to keep the longing for France alive – including the south-west

Regardless of whether you are still researching your trip or are already on the French Atlantic Coast: these addresses will provide you with more information, videos and networks to make your holiday even more enjoyable

http://fr-fr.facebook.com/gitesde-france.landes.sudouest On Facebook: information about small, personally run places to stay in the southwest of France

www.telegraph.co.uk/travel/destinations/europe/france/8526267/Camping-in-France-Perfect-pitches-on-the-Atlantic-coast.html A personal selection of campsites down the Atlantic coast

twitter.com/SO_Paysbasque The latest from the Basque Country with hourly updates from the daily newspaper Sud Ouest

www.viewsurf.com Website with links to countless webcams at surfing hotspots in the whole of France, incl. more than 100 on the French Atlantic Coast

VIDEOS

short.travel/fra3 A collection of videos from Biarritz Aquarium

short.travel/fra4 The best slapstick from Jacques Tati's legendary film "Monsieur Hulot's Holiday"

short.travel/fra2 The webcam shows the waves off the lovely bay of Biarritz – the camera pans over all the beaches

APPS

Bordeaux Aquitaine Wine Trip Addresses of castles, wine merchants, vintners and wine bars, plus sights and activities all over the growing area

Royan tour A guided tour of Royan with addresses and information on restaurants, accommodation, beaches, events, etc

Girondins Officiel For football fans who need their daily dose of sport! All you need to know about the team from Bordeaux

The world-class wines of Médoc near Bordeaux General information about the big names in the area, tips for visits to châteaux and what to order when dining

TRAVEL TIPS

ACCOMMODATION

The spectrum of accommodation facilities on the French Atlantic Coast ranges from youth hostels (information: *FUAJ | tel. 01 44 89 87 27 | www.fuaj.org*) and *chambres d'hôtes* – which are the French equivalent to Bed & Breakfast –, to luxury hotels. In summer – and especially during the French school holidays, usually in July and August – advance booking is absolutely essential. In many hotels on the Atlantic coast there is a minimum stay of 1 week in the high season; for holiday flats and cottages this is often even raised to 2 weeks in July/August.

ADMISSION PRICES

Average admission prices to sights such as museums, gardens, *châteaux* and

RESPONSIBLE TRAVEL

It doesn't take a lot to be environmentally friendly whilst travelling. Don't just think about your carbon footprint whilst flying to and from your holiday destination but also about how you can protect nature and culture abroad. As a tourist it is especially important to respect nature, look out for local products, cycle instead of driving, save water and much more. If you would like to find out more about eco-tourism please visit: *www.ecotourism.org*

other tourist attractions are between 3.50 and 8 euros for adults with children paying around half. Amusement parks are considerably more expensive. There are concessions (50 %) for students with a valid international student pass in museums.

ARRIVAL

Crossing the Channel from England, the best route from Calais to the French Atlantic Coast is via Paris and then on the A11 motorway Paris–Le Mans–Nantes (384 km/239 mi) or on the A10 via Tours and Poitiers to La Rochelle or Bordeaux (560 km/348 mi). Alternatively, if you cross to Le Havre or Cherbourg, it is best to head for Le Mans or Rennes respectively. If you are going to the Basque Country, the long crossing from Plymouth to Bilbao in Spain may be a viable alternative.

The high-speed train, TGV, covers the distance Paris–Nantes in 2 hours, Paris–Bordeaux in 3. The Eurotunnel shuttle service between Folkestone and Calais operates 365 days a year with up to 4 departures an hour *(www.euro tunnel.com/uk/home)*. Those who are travelling to the Côte d'Argent and Côte Basque can take the TGV to the Spanish border. Advance reservation necessary.

A number of national as well as budget airlines fly from various major and provincial UK airports to Bordeaux and Nantes, as well as Biarritz, Pau and Bergerac. It is worth spending some time looking for the best connections and comparing prices, e.g. under *www.flybe.com*,

From arrival to weather

Your holiday from start to finish: the most important addresses and information for your trip to the French Atlantic Coast

www.easyjet.co.uk, www.britishairways. com (e.g. Gatwick–Bordeaux) and *www. airfrance.co.uk* (e.g. Heathrow–Pau), or ask your local travel agent.

BANKS & CREDIT CARDS

Cashpoint terminals (ATMs) can be found on virtually every corner (for EC and credit cards). Credit cards are widely accepted in hotels, restaurants, shops and garages in France (esp. Visa and Eurocard), even for smaller amounts.

CAMPING

Campsites of all categories are two a penny. In the forests and dunes on the Côte d'Argent in particular, one site rubs shoulders with the next. Nevertheless, reservations are necessary in the high season. An overview of all campsites (plus links) can be found on the website of the Fédération Française de Camping et de Caravaning: *ffcc.fr*; the Société France Com lists campingsites on *www. camping-france.com*

CAR HIRE

Major car hire companies can be found at the airports and in larger towns and cities. A driving licence – which you must have held for at least 1 year – has to be presented. It is almost always cheaper hiring a car and organising insurance before travelling, especially in the high season (e.g. *www.autoeurope. eu*). On arrival always check the car for scratches or dents and make sure the tank has been filled up. Avoid taking out additional insurance – this is generally superfluous and can lead to unnecessary costs.

CONSULATES & EMBASSIES

BRITISH CONSULATE
353, Blvd. du Président Wilson | 33073 Bordeaux | tel. +33 5 57 22 21 10 | ukin france.fco.gov.uk/en

CONSULATE OF THE UNITED STATES OF AMERICA
89, Quai des Chartrons | 33300 Bordeaux | tel. +33 5 56 48 63 85 | bordeaux. usconsulate.gov

CUSTOMS

UK citizens do not have to pay any duty on goods brought from another EU country as long as tax was included in the price and the items are for private consumption only. Tax free allowances include: 800 cigarettes, 400 cigarillos, 200 cigars, 1kg/2.2lbs pipe tobacco, 10L spirits, 20L liqueurs, 90L wine, 110L beer. Those travelling from the USA, Canada, Australia or other non-EU countries are allowed to enter with the following tax-free amounts: 200 cigarettes or 100 cigarillos or 50 cigars or 250g pipe tobacco. 2L wine and spirits with less than 22 vol. % alcohol, 1L spirits with more than 22 vol. % alcohol content.

American passport holders returning to the USA do not have to pay duty on articles purchased overseas up to the value of $800, but there are limits on the amount of alcoholic beverages and tobacco products. For regulations for international travel for U.S. residents see *www.cbp.gov*.

DRIVING

Apart from a few sections, French motorways are tolled. You pay at the *péage* stations, in cash or by card. A toll calculator on the website *www.autoroutes.fr* tells you what charges have to be paid on your planned route if you enter your starting point and destination under 'Votre Itinéraire'. If you break down, emergency phones are 2 km/1.25 mi apart. Main roads *(routes nationales)* are generally good but correspondingly heavily used. Speed limits: 130 km/h/80 mph on motorways (110 km/h/68 mph when raining); 110 km/h/68 mph on dual carriageways; 90 km/h/55 mph on routes nationales and routes départementales (80 km/h/49 mph when raining); 50 km/h/30 mph in built-up areas. Motorbikes must have dipped headlights on at all times; this also applies to all other vehicles when raining or foggy. You are required by law to carry a reflective (hi-vis) safety vest for the driver and each of the passengers in the car. In France, it is against the law to use and even to carry mobile or integrated navigation systems with radar detectors. If you are caught with one, you must expect a heavy fine and to have the device confiscated.

EMERGENCY SERVICES

The emergency number is *tel. 112*

HEALTH

If you are a UK resident, before going abroad apply for a free European Health Insurance Card (EHIC) from the NHS which allows you access to medical treatment while travelling. It is worth noting that the new European health card is not (yet) being accepted by doctors in France as French card machines are only set for the local plastic cards. Private medical travel insurance is highly recommended.

IMMIGRATION

A valid passport is required for entry into France. All children must travel with their own passport. Citizens of EU countries, the USA and Canada do not need visas to visit France as tourists for a stay of less than three months.

INFORMATION

ATOUT FRANCE – FRENCH TOURISM DEVELOPMENT AGENCY

– Lincoln House, 296–300 High Holborn | London WC1V 7JH | tel. 207 061 66 00 | www.atout-france.fr; www.rendezvousenfrance.com

REGIONAL TOURIST INFORMATION OFFICES

– Pays de la Loire (Côte d'Amour): 7, Rue du Général de Bollardière | 44202 Nantes | tel. 02 40 89 89 89 | www. enpaysdelaloire.com

– Vendée (Côte de Lumière): 45, Blvd. des États-Unis | 85000 La Roche-sur-Yon | tel. 02 51 47 88 20 | www.vendee-tourisme.com

– Charente-Maritime (Côte de Lumière): 85, Blvd. de la République | 17076 La Rochelle | tel. 05 46 31 71 71 | www.en-charente-maritime.com

– Gironde (Côte d'Argent, Bordelais): 9, Rue Fodaudège | 33000 Bordeaux | tel. 05 56 52 61 40 | www.tourisme-gironde.fr

– Landes (Côte d'Argent): 4, Av. Aristide Briand | 40012 Mont-de-Marsan | tel. 05 58 06 89 89 | www.tourismelandes.com

– *Béarn-Pays Basque (Côte Basque): 2, Allées des Platanes | 64100 Bayonne | tel. 05 59 30 01 30 | www.tourisme64.com*

INFORMATION WEBSITES

Most websites of the tourist information offices in towns and cities as well as regional sites are also in English. These provide practical tips and comprehensive information on what to see and where to stay. Films/videos and live webcams give a good impression of the various holiday destinations. The following websites provide useful general information:

– *www.frenchatlantic.worldweb.com:* practical travel tips with tourism directory, tours, events, accommodation, sights, etc.

– *http://about-france.com/tourism/french-seaside-coast.htm:* information on the coastlines and beaches in France in general with a section on the Atlantic coast

– *www.france-atlantic.com/charente/la-rochelle-tourist-information.asp:* information on La Rochelle and the Charente-Maritime département

– *www.bordeaux-tourisme.com/index_uk.html:* comprehensive information website on the World Heritage Site, wine-tasting, practical and cultural information

INTERNET ACCESS & WI-FI

In France, there is normally free WiFi access in hotels, restaurants, museums and lots of shops. As elsewhere in Europe, you can also access the Internet free at airports and in many other public places.

By contrast, it is almost impossible to find Internet cafés anywhere anymore.

MOSQUITOES

Mosquitoes can be a nuisance in the evenings especially on lakes and rivers inland but also sometimes on the coast too. Mosquito repellent is a must in your luggage.

BUDGETING

Coffee	from £ 2.70 / $ 3.70 *for a café crème*
Ice cream	£ 1.30–2.20 /$ 1.80–3 *per scoop*
Wine	from £ 2.20/$ 3 *for a glass*
Souvenirs	around £ 11.50–13.50 / $ 16–18.50 *for a typical Basque striped towel*
Petrol	around £ 1.20 /$ 1.65 *for 1 litre of Super 95*
Bicycle	£ 9–11 /$ 12.50–15 *daily hire charge*

MOTOR HOMES

There are plenty of campsites along the Atlantic coast, and it is the perfect destination for a holiday in a motor home. There are 3700 approved motor home sites on car parks and 1600 campsites that can accommodate motor homes. Parking may be problematic, though, even if lots of towns offer parking for motor homes. You can download the "Guide Camp'in France FFCC" at *www.ffcc.fr* (heading "Camping Car", then "Camp'in France").

NUDISM

Naturisme, as the French call it, is very popular in France. On the Côte d'Argent in particular there are lots of nudist holiday complexes. These *domaines*

naturistes are usually well equipped campsites, some with bungalows to rent, with sports and leisure facilities. In other areas, there are virtually always sections of the beach or bay where nude bathing is tolerated. These are, however, often not manned by lifeguards.

OPENING HOURS

In the low season small museums in particular are only open on certain days or by prior appointment.

PERSONAL SAFETY

Normal precautions – like anywhere else in the world – should be taken. Don't leave valuables in parked vehicles and be careful of pickpockets (also on the beach).

PHONE & MOBILE PHONE

Most of the few telephone boxes that do still exist are card phones. A *télécarte* can be bought at tobacconists, post offices and garages. The west of France is covered by several mobile phone networks. Ask your provider which French network is the cheapest for your needs and switch over to this manually if another, more expensive partner is selected automatically. Prepaid cards can also be bought at post offices and tobacconists. These often work out cheaper. Text messaging is always cheap. Mailboxes cause high costs – you should switch off this function. The international code for calling France from abroad is *+33*. To call other countries, dial the country code (UK *+44*, US *+1*, Ireland *+353*), and then the telephone number without *0*.

WEATHER IN THE MÉDOC

	Jan	Feb	March	April	May	June	July	Aug	Sept	Oct	Nov	Dec
Daytime temperatures in °C/°F												
	9/48	11/52	15/59	17/63	20/68	24/75	25/77	26/79	23/73	18/64	13/55	9/48
Night-time temperatures in °C/°F												
	2/36	2/36	4/39	6/43	9/48	12/54	14/57	14/57	12/54	8/46	5/41	3/37
☀	3	4	6	7	8	8	8	8	7	5	3	2
☂	16	13	13	13	14	11	11	12	13	14	15	17
〰	10/50	10/50	10/50	11/52	13/55	15/59	17/63	17/63	16/61	15/59	13/55	11/52

POST

Letters and postcards to EU countries cost 1 euro. *www.laposte.fr.* You can also buy stamps from tobacconists when you purchase a postcard.

PUBLIC TRANSPORT

In Nantes, La Rochelle and Bordeaux, trams, buses, ferries and electric vehicle rental points are very well organised. Environmental awareness is high. Free use of public transport is included in the tourist passes for the towns that offer reduced or free entrance to the sights. However, you will probably need a car in rural areas. You can hire bicycles almost everywhere. To save taking a car on a ferry, bikes can be rented everywhere. Regional trains (TER) operate between urban centres as do coaches run by the French railway company, SNCF. *www.voyages-sncf.co.uk*

TAXI

Taxis are not any one colour in France but must have a 'Taxi' sign on the roof. If it is lit up, the taxi is for hire. Different fares apply at night. Check fare prices under: *www.taxis-de-france.com*

TIPPING

Add up to 10% to the bill in a restaurant and to a taxi fare. Tips are left in hotels for particularly attentive service. If staying anywhere for a long period, chambermaids are usually given a tip of 10–20 euros a week.

TOURIST TAX

An obligatory *taxe de séjour* is added to the room price in hotels in holiday resorts. This is normally 50 cents–1.50 euro per person, per night.

WEATHER, WHEN TO GO

Everyone in France is out and about from mid July until the beginning of Sept. This is the fullest, hottest and most expensive time of year, and it is absolutely essential to book accommodation in advance. Between June–Sept the Atlantic is warm enough to swim in; the hardy start swimming in May. If you can, travel in the low season. In late autumn, prices drop considerably. This is an ideal time for wine trips, thalossotherapy and city sightseeing.

CURRENCY CONVERTER

£	€	€	£
1	1.10	1	0.90
3	3.30	3	2.70
5	5.50	5	4.50
13	14.30	13	11.70
40	44	40	36
75	82.50	75	67.50
120	132	120	108
250	275	250	225
500	550	500	450

$	€	€	$
1	0.80	1	1.25
3	2.40	3	3.75
5	4	5	6.25
13	10.40	13	16.25
40	32	40	50
75	60	75	93.75
120	96	120	250
250	200	250	312.50
500	400	500	625

For current exchange rates see www.xe.com

USEFUL PHRASES FRENCH

IN BRIEF

Yes/No/Maybe	oui/non/peut-être
Please/Thank you	s'il vous plaît/merci
Good morning!/afternoon!/ evening!/night!	Bonjour!/Bonjour!/ Bonsoir!/Bonne nuit!
Hello!/goodbye!/See you!	Salut!/Au revoir!/Salut!
Excuse me, please	Pardon!
My name is ...	Je m'appelle ...
I'm from ...	Je suis de ...
May I ...?/ Pardon?	Puis-je ...?/Comment?
I would like to .../have you got ...?	Je voudrais .../Avez-vous?
How much is ...?	Combien coûte ...?
I (don't) like this	Ça (ne) me plaît (pas).
good/bad/broken	bon/mauvais/cassé
too much/much/little	trop/beaucoup/peu
all/nothing	tout/rien
Help!/Attention!	Au secours/attention
police/fire brigade/ambulance	police/pompiers/ambulance
Could you please help me?	Est-ce que vous pourriez m'aider?
Do you speak English?	Parlez-vous anglais?
Do you understand?	Est-ce que vous comprenez?
Could you please ...?	Pourriez vous ... s'il vous plait?
... repeat that	répéter
... speak more slowly	parler plus lentement
... write that down	l'écrire

DATE & TIME

Monday/Tuesday	lundi/mardi
Wednesday/Thursday	mercredi/jeudi
Friday/Saturday/Sunday	vendredi/samedi/dimanche
working day/holiday	jour ouvrable/jour férié
today/tomorrow/yesterday	aujourd'hui /demain/hier
hour/minute	heure/minute
day/night/week	jour/nuit/semaine
month/year	mois/année
What time is it?	Quelle heure est-t-il?
	Il est trois heures
It's half past three.	Il est trois heures et demi
a quarter to four	quatre heures moins le quart

Parlez-vous français?

"Do you speak French?" This guide will help you to say the basic words and phrases in French

TRAVEL

open/closed	ouvert/fermé
entrance/exit	entrée/sortie
departure/arrival	départ/arrivée
toilets/restrooms /	toilettes/
ladies/gentlemen	femmes/hommes
(no) drinking water	eau (non) potable
Where is ...?/Where are ...?	Où est ...?/Où sont ...?
left/right	à gauche/à droite
straight ahead/back	tout droit/en arrière
close/far	près/loin
bus/tram/underground / taxi/cab	bus/tramway/métro/taxi
stop/cab stand	arrêt/station de taxi
parking lot/parking garage	parking
street map/map	plan de ville/carte routière
train station/harbour/	gare/port/
airport	aéroport
schedule/ticket	horaire/billet
single/return	aller simple/aller-retour
train/track/platform	train/voie/quai
I would like to rent ...	Je voudrais ... louer.
a car/a bicycle/	une voiture/un vélo/
a boat	un bateau

FOOD & DRINK

The menu, please	La carte, s'il vous plaît.
Could I please have ...?	Puis-je avoir ... s'il vous plaît
bottle/carafe/glass	bouteille/carafe/verre
knife/fork/spoon	couteau/fourchette/cuillère
salt/pepper/sugar	sel/poivre/sucre
vinegar/oil	vinaigre/huile
milk/cream/lemon	lait/crême/citron
cold/too salty/not cooked	froid/trop salé/pas cuit
with/without ice/sparkling	avec/sans glaçons/gaz
vegetarian	végétarien(ne)
May I have the bill, please	Je voudrais payer, s'il vous plaît
bill	addition

SHOPPING

pharmacy/chemist	pharmacie/droguerie
baker/market	boulangerie/marché
shopping centre	centre commercial
department store	grand magasin
100 grammes/1 kilo	cent grammes/un kilo
expensive/cheap/price	cher/bon marché/prix
more/less	plus/moins
organically grown	de l'agriculture biologique

ACCOMMODATION

I have booked a room	J'ai réservé une chambre
Do you have any ... left?	Avez-vous encore ...?
single room/double room	chambre simple/double
breakfast	petit déjeuner
half board/	demi-pension/
full board (American plan)	pension complète
shower/sit-down bath	douche/bain
balcony/terrace	balcon /terrasse
key/room card	clé/carte magnétique
luggage/suitcase/bag	bagages/valise/sac

BANKS, MONEY & CREDIT CARDS

bank/ATM/pin code	banque/guichet automatique/code
cash/credit card	comptant/carte de crédit
bill/coin	billet/monnaie

HEALTH

doctor/dentist/paediatrician	médecin/dentiste/pédiatre
hospital/emergency clinic	hôpital/urgences
fever/pain	fièvre/douleurs
diarrhoea/nausea	diarrhée/nausée
sunburn	coup de soleil
inflamed/injured	enflammé/blessé
plaster/bandage	pansement/bandage
ointment/pain reliever	pommade/analgésique

POST, TELECOMMUNICATIONS & MEDIA

stamp	timbre
lettre/postcard	lettre/carte postale
I need a landline phone card	J'ai besoin d'une carte téléphonique pour fixe.
I'm looking for a prepaid card for my mobile	Je cherche une recharge pour mon portable.
Where can I find internet access?	Où puis-je trouver un accès à internet?
dial/connection/engaged	composer/connection/occupé
socket/charger	prise électrique/chargeur
computer/battery/rechargeable battery	ordinateur/batterie/accumulateur
at sign (@)	arobase
internet address (URL)/ e-mail address	adresse internet/ mail
internet connection/wifi	accès internet/wi-fi
e-mail/file/print	mail/fichier/imprimer

LEISURE, SPORTS & BEACH

beach	plage
sunshade/lounger	parasol/transat
low tide/high tide/current	marée basse/marée haute/courant
cable car/chair lift	téléphérique/télésiège
(rescue) hut	refuge

NUMBERS

0	zéro	17	dix-sept
1	un, une	18	dix-huit
2	deux	19	dix-neuf
3	trois	20	vingt
4	quatre	30	trente
5	cinq	40	quarante
6	six	50	cinquante
7	sept	60	soixante
8	huit	70	soixante-dix
9	neuf	80	quatre-vingt
10	dix	90	quatre-vingt-dix
11	onze	100	cent
12	douze	200	deux cents
13	treize	1000	mille
14	quatorze		
15	quinze	½	un[e] demi[e]
16	seize	¼	un quart

ROAD ATLAS

The green line indicates the Discovery Tour
„French Atlantic Coast at a glance"
The blue line indicates the other Discovery Tours
All tours are also marked on the pull-out map

Exploring the French Atlantic Coast

The map on the back cover shows how
the area has been sub-divided

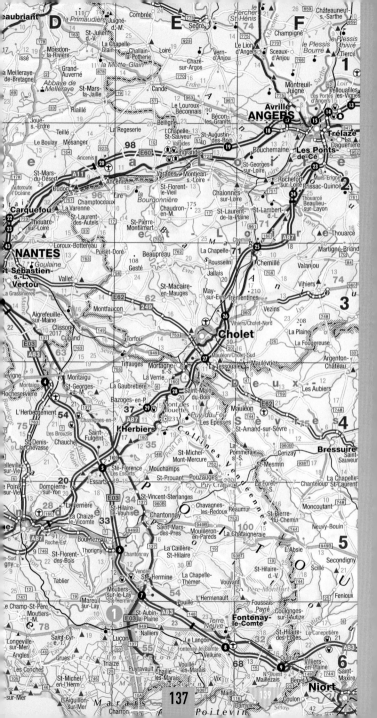

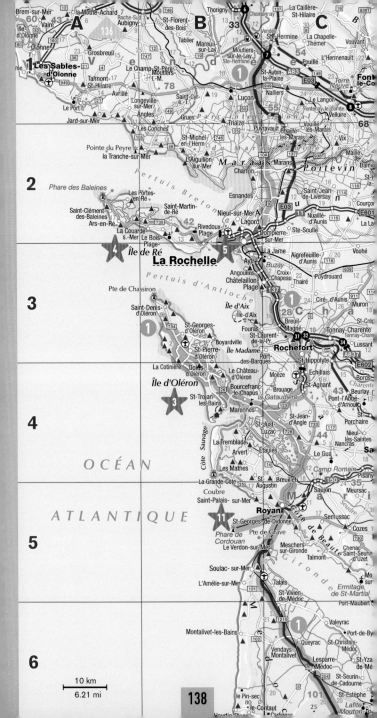

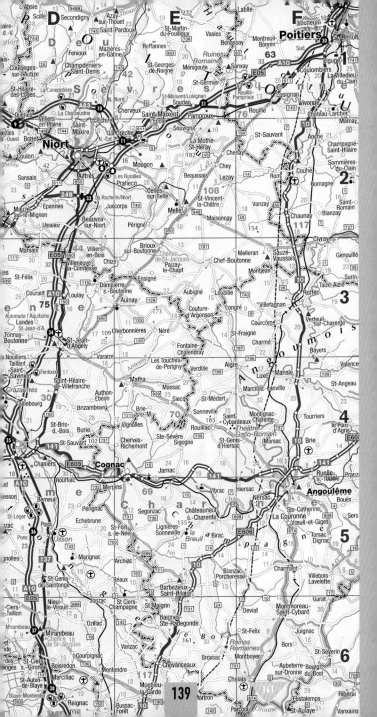

139

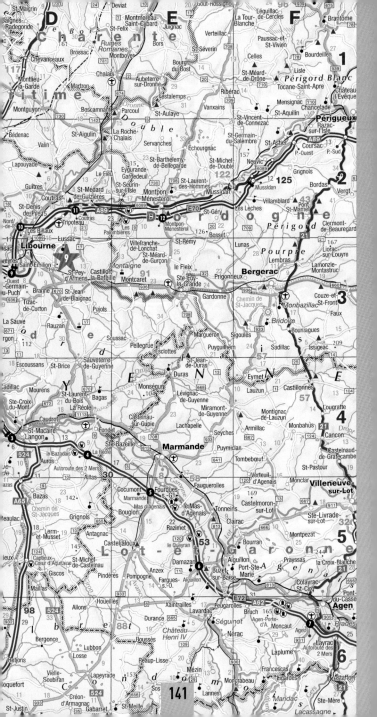

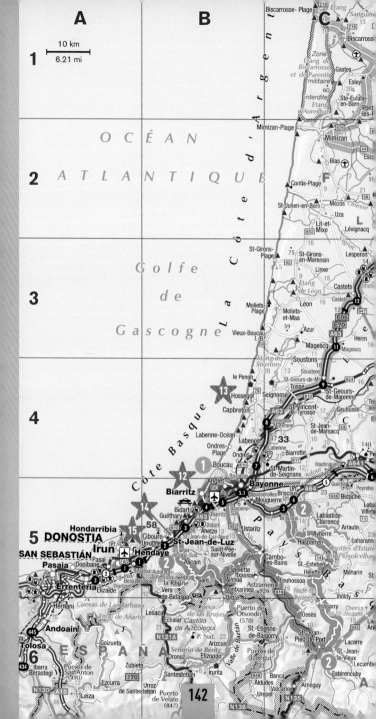

A

10 km
6.21 mi

B

C

OCÉAN

ATLANTIQUE

Biscarrosse-Plage
Étang
Sanguine
216
Biscarrosse
Zone
Étang de
Biscarrosse
et de Parentis
militaire
60
interdite
Étang
d'Aureilhan
Ste-Eulalie-en-Born
Gastes
Esleys
Pont
les-B

Mimizan-Plage
Mimizan
Bias
Esco

Contis-Plage
Mézos
Onesse
St-Julien-en-Born
Uza
Lit-et-Mixe
Lévignacq

Golfe

de

Gascogne

St-Girons-Plage
St-Girons-en-Marensin
Linxe
Lesperon
Castets
Étang
de Léon
Castets
Chen
Moliets-Plage
Léon
Moliets-et-Maa
Azur
Vieux-Boucau-l.-B
Magescq
Herm
Magescq
Étang de
Soustons
Soustons
St-Geours-de-M
Tosse
le Penon
Seignosse
St-Geours-de-Maremne
Hossegor
St-Vincent-Tyrosse
Saubusse
Capbreton
Bénesse-Maremne
St-Jean-de-Marsacq
Labenne-Océan
33
Labenne
Ondres-Plage
Biarrotte
Ondres
St-Martin-de-Seignanx
Boucau
Hastingue
Anglet
Bayonne
Peyreho
Biarritz
Mousserolles Briscous
Bidart
Mouguerre
Urt
Bidache
Guéthary
Bayonne-Sud
Briscous
Labastide-Clairence
St-Jean-de-Luz-Nord
Ahetze
Ustaritz
Ayherre
Arraute
Hondarribia
St-Jean-de-Luz
Cambo-les-Bains
Hasparren
Laharann
DONOSTIA
Irun
St-Jean-de-Luz-Sud
Ascain
Saint-Pée-sur-Nivelle
Espelette
Itxassou
St-Esteben
Méharin
SAN SEBASTIÁN
Hendaye
Urrugne
Ciboure
Sare
Ainhoa
Louhossoa
Hélette
Iholdy
Pasaia
Donibane
Vera de Bidasoa
la Rhune
Artzamendi
Irissarry
Errenteria
Elizalde
Bera/Bidasoa
Urdax
Route de
Pyrénées
Chemin
St-Jacques
Hernani
Oiartzun
Lesaca
Cueva
de las Brujas
St-Étienne-de-Baïgorry
Lacarre
Andoain
Goizueta
Echalar
Castillo de Aizcolegui
Puerto de Otsondo
Ossès
St-Jean-Pied-de-Port
St-Jean-le-Vieux
Tolosa
Ibarra
Berastegi
Puerto de San Antón
Zubieta
P. Nat.
Arizcun
Elizondo
Valle de Baztán
Puerto de Ispegui
Lecumbe
La An
ESPAÑA
Ezcurra
Urroz
de Santesteban
Santesteban
Irurita
Aldudes
Valcarlos
Urepel
Estérençuby
Leiza
Puerto de Velate
Banca
Arneguy

142

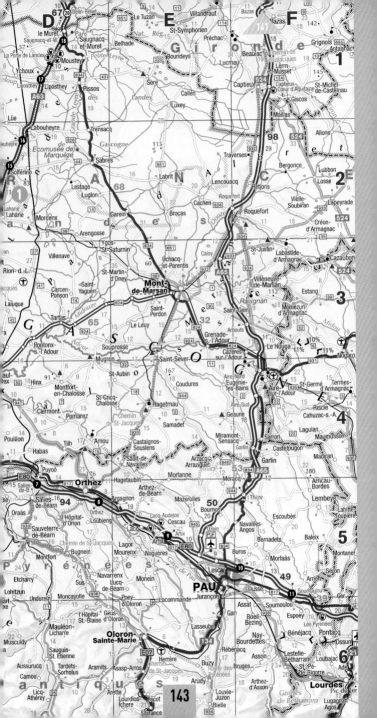

KEY TO ROAD ATLAS

Autobahn mit Anschlussstellen Motorway with junctions	
Autobahn in Bau Motorway under construction	
Mautstelle Toll station	
Raststätte mit Übernachtung Roadside restaurant and hotel	
Raststätte Roadside restaurant	
Tankstelle Filling-station	
Autobahnähnliche Schnell- straße mit Anschlussstelle Dual carriage-way with motorway characteristics with junction	
Fernverkehrsstraße Trunk road	
Durchgangsstraße Thoroughfare	
Wichtige Hauptstraße Important main road	
Hauptstraße Main road	
Nebenstraße Secondary road	
Eisenbahn Railway	
Autozug-Terminal Car-loading terminal	
Zahnradbahn Mountain railway	
Kabinenschwebebahn Aerial cableway	
Eisenbahnfähre Railway ferry	
Autofähre Car ferry	
Schifffahrtslinie Shipping route	
Landschaftlich besonders schöne Strecke Route with beautiful scenery	
Alleenstr. Touristenstraße Tourist route	
XI-V Wintersperre Closure in winter	
Straße für Kfz gesperrt Road closed to motor traffic	
8% Bedeutende Steigungen Important gradients	
Für Wohnwagen nicht empfehlenswert Not recommended for caravans	
Für Wohnwagen gesperrt Closed for caravans	
Besonders schöner Ausblick Important panoramic view	

Wartenstein Sehenswert: Kultur - Natur *Umbalfälle* Of interest: culture - nature	
Badestrand Bathing beach	
Nationalpark, Naturpark National park, nature park	
Sperrgebiet Prohibited area	
Kirche Church	
Kloster Monastery	
Schloss, Burg Palace, castle	
Moschee Mosque	
Ruinen Ruins	
Leuchtturm Lighthouse	
Turm Tower	
Höhle Cave	
Ausgrabungsstätte Archaeological excavation	
Jugendherberge Youth hostel	
Allein stehendes Hotel Isolated hotel	
Berghütte Refuge	
Campingplatz Camping site	
Flughafen Airport	
Regionalflughafen Regional airport	
Flugplatz Airfield	
Staatsgrenze National boundary	
Verwaltungsgrenze Administrative boundary	
Grenzkontrollstelle Check-point	
Grenzkontrollstelle mit Beschränkung Check-point with restrictions	
ROMA Hauptstadt Capital	
VENEZIA Verwaltungssitz Seat of the administration	
MARCO POLO Erlebnistour 1 MARCO POLO Discovery Tour 1	
MARCO POLO Erlebnistouren MARCO POLO Discovery Tours	
MARCO POLO Highlight MARCO POLO Highlight	

FOR YOUR NEXT TRIP...

MARCO POLO TRAVEL GUIDES

Travel with
Insider
Tips

INDEX

This index lists all sights and destinations featured in this guide.
Numbers in bold indicate a main entry.

CREDITS

WRITE TO US

e-mail: info@marcopologuides.co.uk

Did you have a great holiday?
Is there something on your mind?
Whatever it is, let us know!
Whether you want to praise, alert us
to errors or give us a personal tip –
MARCO POLO would be pleased to
hear from you.
We do everything we can to provide the
very latest information for your trip.

Nevertheless, despite all of our authors'
thorough research, errors can creep in.
MARCO POLO does not accept any
liability for this. Please contact us by
e-mail or post.

MARCO POLO Travel Publishing Ltd
Pinewood, Chineham Business Park
Crockford Lane, Chineham
Basingstoke, Hampshire RG24 8AL
United Kingdom

PICTURE CREDITS
Cover photograph: Beach in Soulac-sur-Mer (Laif/hemis.fr: E. Bouloumie)
Photos: W. Dieterich (122 top); DuMont Bildarchiv: Huber (120/121); © fotolia.com/kentoh (18 bottom); Getty Images: M. Shen (29); Guily fish spa (19 top); huber-images: F. Carovillano (55, 96/97), Gräfenhain (flap left, 84/85), F. Olimpio (76), Stadler (122 bottom); © iStockphoto: Adam Dodd (18 top); Laif: Amme (9), C. Boisvieux (106), J.-P. Bouchard (25), Heuer (30/31), Knechtel (8); Laif/Gamma-RaphoA: H. Champollion (46/47); Laif/hemis: J.-D. Soudres (61); Laif/hemis.fr: J.-P. Azam (57), J.-M. Barrere (71), E. Berthier (110), E. Bouloumie (1 top), A. Chicurel (74), F. Guiziou (4 top, 32/33, 37), J.-M. Liot (4 bottom, 26/27), Rieger (10), P. Roy (121); Laif/Le Figaro Magazine: R. Escher (86), Mazodier (68/69), Prignet (48, 52); Laif/Madame Figaro: G. Bretzel (30); Laif/REA: L. Cerino (63), R. Damoret (14/15), J. C. Thuillier (79); Laif/robertharding: J. Elliott (73); Laif/Tama: Rossi (120); Laif/Tripelon: Jarry (34); Le Saint Sabastien: Richard Duart (18 centre); Lookphotos: B. Merz (17); Lookphotos/age fotostock (64/65, 83, 103); Lookphotos/Hemis (43, 95); Lookphotos/SagaPhoto (93); mauritius images: R. Mattes (39), K. Neuner (20/21); mauritius images/age fotostock: D. Chang (flap right); mauritius images/Alamy (11, 19 bottom), J. Alba (6, 66), N. Calvo (5, 112/113), N. Hanna (119), S. Reddy (28 left); mauritius images/foodcollection (28 right); mauritius images/Hemis.fr: P. Jacques (31, 90), H. Lenain (58, 108/109), F. Leroy (115); mauritius images/imagebroker: L. McKie (40); mauritius images/John Warburton-Lee: S. Egan (12/13), J. Warburton Lee (2, 51); mauritius images/Photo Alto (116/117); mauritius images/Photononstop: G. Guittot (81), J. Loic (45); mauritius images/Westend61/JuNi Art (7); mauritius images/Westend61/U. Umstätter (3); T. Stankiewicz (23, 89, 123); E. Wrba (134/135)

2nd edition 2019 – fully updated and revised
Worldwide Distribution: Marco Polo Travel Publishing Ltd, Pinewood, Chineham Business Park,
Crockford Lane, Basingstoke, Hampshire RG24 8AL, United Kingdom. Email: sales@marcopolouk.com
© MAIRDUMONT GmbH & Co. KG, Ostfildern
Chief editor: Marion Zorn; Author: Stefanie Bisping; editor: Nikolai Michaelis
Programme supervision: Stephan Dürr, Lucas Forst-Gill, Susanne Heimburger, Nikolai Michaelis, Martin Silbermann, Kristin Wittemann; Picture editors: Gabriele Forst, Stefanie Wiese
What's hot: wunder media, Munich
Cartography road atlas & pull-out map: © MAIRDUMONT, Ostfildern
Cover design, p. 1, pull-out map cover: Karl Anders – Büro für Visual Stories, Hamburg; design inside: milchhof:atelier, Berlin; design p. 2/3, Discovery Tours: Susan Chaaban Dipl.-Des. (FH)
Translated from German by Christopher Wynne and Mo Croasdale
Editorial office: SAW Communications, Redaktionsbüro Dr. Sabine A. Werner, Mainz: Julia Gilcher, Cosima Talhouni, Dr. Sabine A. Werner; prepress: SAW Communications, Mainz, in cooperation with alles mit Medien, Mainz
Phrase book in cooperation with Ernst Klett Sprachen GmbH, Stuttgart, Editorial by Pons Wörterbücher

MIX
Paper from
responsible sources
FSC® C124385

DOS & DON'TS ✋

A few things to bear in mind on the French Atlantic Coast

DON'T DROP CIGARETTE ENDS

Forest fires are a real threat in south-west France in particular due to the extensive pine forests. You should be exceptionally careful with matches, cigarette ends and fire in general.

DO TRY TO SPEAK A BIT OF FRENCH

Even if you can't speak much of the language, a polite *'Bonjour, Madame'* or *'Bonjour, Monsieur'* always goes down well and will help you get on with everyone you meet.

DON'T LET DOGS RUN LOOSE ON THE BEACH

Dogs are often only tolerated on many of the supervised beaches in the early morning or in the evening. Keep an eye out for signs/notices. In other places on the coast dogs are allowed to run off the lead.

DO DROP IN ON WINE PRODUCERS

The cellar door is almost always open to visitors who want to taste a wine-grower's produce. The big exception is during the grape-picking season when visits can interrupt their work.

DON'T UNDERESTIMATE THE POWER OF THE ATLANTIC

Even when the weather is nice and the sea looks calm there are many places on the Atlantic coast where strong undercurrents can put even experienced swimmers in danger. Only go for a swim from beaches with lifeguards *(plages surveillées)* and look at the colour of the flags flying. Green = no danger. Yellow/orange = swimming is dangerous but there is a lifeguard on duty *(poste de surveillance)*. Red = swimming prohibited. Blue flags mark the area being watched. Both incoming and outgoing tides can be treacherous all down the coast. The tide can go out very fast and has a strong pull. When it comes in, it moves quite speedily – basically at walking pace. If you happen to be on a sandbank (which you may not even have realised), you can get cut off very quickly, especially if the water runs in channels *(baines)*. Pay attention to signs at all times.

DON'T ATTACK A CHEESEBOARD

When offered a cheeseboard either in a restaurant or a private house, don't hack off little bits here and there but cut proper wedge-shaped pieces!